insight text guide

Sue Tweg

Richard III

William Shakespeare

insight

innovative engaging evolving

First published in 2007, reprinted 2010, 2015, 2022.

Insight Publications Pty Ltd
3/350 Charman Road
Cheltenham VIC 3192
Australia
Tel: +61 3 8571 4950
Fax: +61 3 8571 0257
Email: books@insightpublications.com.au

www.insightpublications.com.au

National Library of Australia Cataloguing-in-Publication entry:
Tweg, Sue.
William Shakespeare's Richard III.
Bibliography.
For secondary school students.
ISBN 9781921088711 (pbk.).
1. Shakespeare, William, 1564-1616. King Richard III.
I. Title.
822.33

Other ISBNs:
9781925316599 (digital)
9781925316605 (bundle: print + digital)

Cover design: The Modern Art Production Group

Printed in Australia by Ligare Book Printers.

contents

CHARACTER MAP

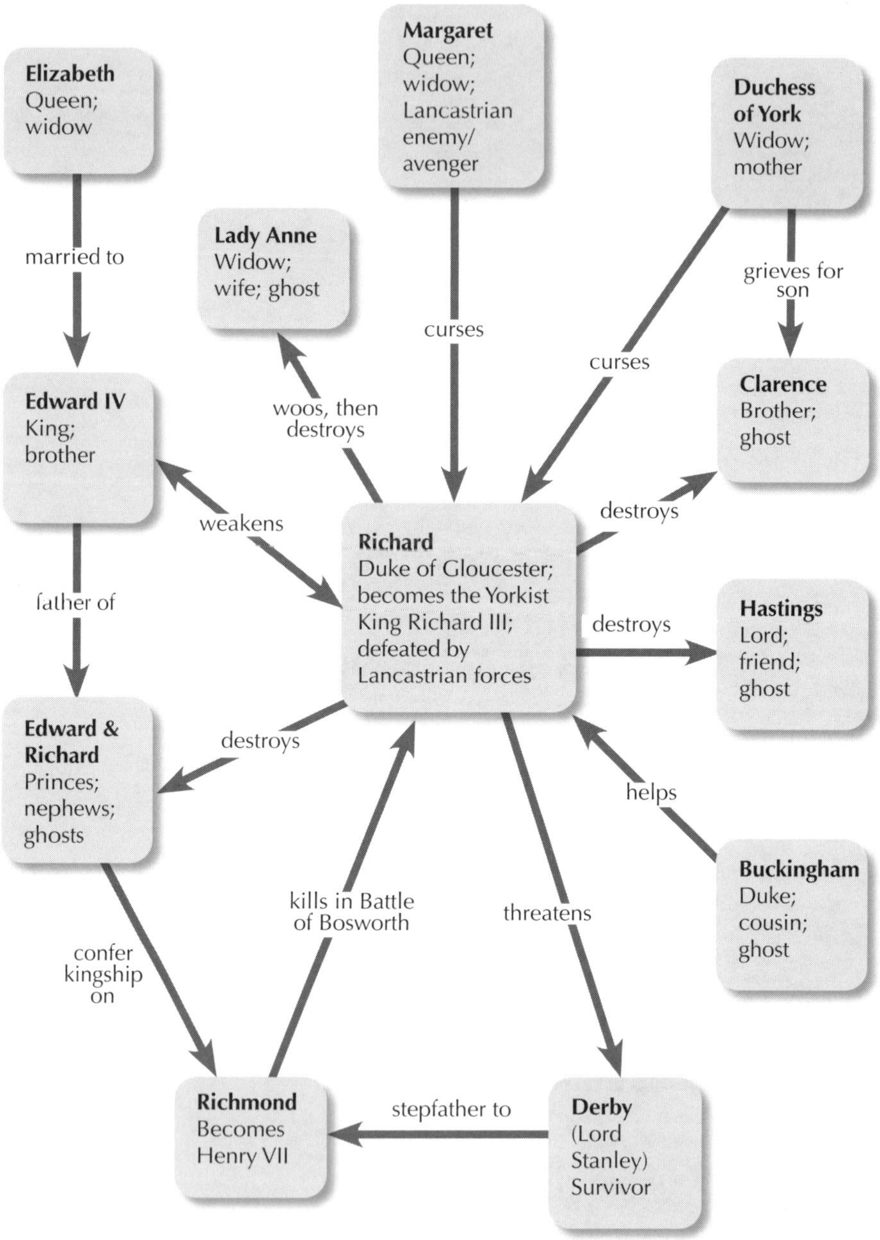

INTRODUCTION

Arch-villain Richard III came to dramatic life first in a latin play at Cambridge a few years before Shakespeare's leading actor, Richard Burbage, took the role to the London stage in the early 1590s. This was early in Shakespeare's career, before the Globe theatre had been built and just over a hundred years since the historical Richard's death in battle.

From the start *The Tragedy of Richard III* was a popular triumph: it was published, probably without Shakespeare's authorisation, at least five times during the playwright's life and then in several versions after, including the First Folio of 1623.

Because these versions are all slightly different from each other, we don't know exactly what Shakespeare's play text might have been. Working with a company in London and travelling around the country, he probably adapted, inserted and cut material to suit the place, actors and situation of the local performance. Modern editions are produced by educated guesswork and choice: they inevitably make Shakespeare seem static, even when they add stage directions. The printed text's unstable history reminds us that Shakespeare wrote it first for actors, to be edited in rehearsal and remembered by individuals doubling several roles.

The play's popularity isn't surprising because it speaks passionately about civil disorder, power politics and tyranny. Londoners of Shakespeare's time could imaginatively put themselves (and their official representative the Lord Mayor) right there in the action. Scenes are dramatically intense, often laced with horror, and mostly dominated by the wickedly attractive personality of Richard himself, the second longest role in Shakespeare (after Hamlet). Richard's energetic villainy and audacious wit propel us through the first three acts – and then the tragic potential in his character emerges to complicate our response to his inevitable fall.

Shakespeare combines English chronicle history and Tudor 'morality' drama to shape a play about divine justice defeating evil personified. Shakespeare's Richard loses his crown because he's a tyrant, in a play that confirms and celebrates the divinely ordained rightness of Tudor inheritance – that is, the legitimacy of Queen Elizabeth I's rule. At the same time, the play's magic takes it beyond simple propaganda: Shakespeare created a fictional Richard whom audiences continue to both love and hate.

BACKGROUND & CONTEXT

Richard III in history

Richard was the last king of the York family line of the Plantagenet dynasty. His rival, Henry Tudor, could trace his ancestry through a shadier line of the same dynasty on the Lancastrian side. Complex relationships in the huge family can be traced in Penguin edition's 'Genealogical Tables' (pp.168–9). Richard and Buckingham were cousins, and both were related to Lady Anne Neville. At the beginning of the family tree, note that Edward III's sons, the Dukes of York and Lancaster, were brothers whose families started the bitter rivalry for the crown.

Shakespeare selects and remixes events from the last two decades of Richard's life. The Wars of the Roses broke out seriously in 1455, when he was under three years old. His family shared the fluctuating fortunes of his father, Richard, Duke of York, as he took over royal power (when Henry VI became incapable through madness). York had a legitimate claim, but Lancastrian opposition was strong and armed conflict inevitable. York's youngest son, seven-year-old Richard, was imprisoned for a time with his mother, the Duchess of York – and then, aged eight, was created Duke of Gloucester when his nineteen-year-old brother Edward became king in 1461, in another surprise reversal of family fortune. Their father York had been mocked by Margaret with a paper crown before being killed less than a year earlier. The young Earl of Rutland, another of Richard's brothers mentioned in the play, had also been killed.

Soon after being crowned, Edward IV married Elizabeth Grey, a Lancastrian widow with children. Richard grew up to be a loyal supporter to his brother and became known as a courageous, well-respected battle leader. The third brother, George, Duke of Clarence, shifted loyalties between the Yorkists and his Lancastrian in-laws, eventually leading to his arrest and execution in 1478. Before his death in 1483, Edward IV appointed Richard as Lord Protector to the royal heir, Prince Edward (a minor).

The last two years of Richard's life (1483–5) were unfortunate at a personal level as well as in the volatile political environment left by Edward's death. Richard might have survived politically, since he was respected and most importantly adult, had he not been deserted by Lord Stanley at the Battle of Bosworth. His long marriage to Anne Neville ended with her wasting death (probably from tuberculosis) early in 1485, less than a year after the death of their frail ten-year-old son. Contemporary reports tell of the almost mad grief the parents experienced.

Richard's disfigurement

Richard is very aware of his limping deformity in the play, using it to gain sympathy or suffering other people's insults (like 'bunch-backed toad', 'bottled spider' and little York's 'ape' wisecrack). If you search the internet for the handful of portraits of Richard III you'll soon find that each one was painted in the Tudor period. Some were over-painted to exaggerate distorted shoulders, arm and hand, make his lips thinner and his eyes narrower. Details of Richard's misshapen body with a mind to match were popularised by Thomas More's 'History' (see 'Shakespeare's Richard' below). There is no contemporary evidence to suggest he was deformed in any way, although his muscular sword-shoulder may have looked hunched on his reportedly small physique.

Princes in the Tower

Prince Edward was over twelve (almost an adult for the times) and Richard of York was ten in 1483, hardly innocent 'babes' as they are repeatedly called to emphasise their vulnerability. No evidence has been found to implicate Richard, the Princes' uncle, in their presumed murder, though they weren't seen in public again after 1484 when rumours of their illegitimacy were circulating. Richard had been proclaimed king by Parliament, not in the devious charade staged for the Mayor and citizens that the play shows.

Shakespeare's plays about the Wars of the Roses

Read the excellent Introduction to this play in the Penguin or Oxford editions for details of Shakespeare's sources (where he found themes, characters and dramatically interesting situations). I also use Geoffrey Bullough's *Narrative and Dramatic Sources of Shakespeare, Vol.III*, which handily gathers together all likely source material, including the latin play.

Shakespeare changes contexts and introduces anachronisms (things inconsistent with the time and place they are placed in) to reshape historical events in Richard's life for maximum effect.

Shakespeare knew from the chronicle histories of Hall and Holinshed that the Wars of the Roses had been catastrophic for England, leaving a bloody trail of division. Henry Tudor's defeat of Richard III and marriage to Elizabeth of York was interpreted as a blessing dropped from heaven at last, reuniting families and establishing what became known as the Tudor Peace. Richard III, cast as the cruel tyrant in this scenario, played a key part in the Tudor attempt to deal out just retribution: to Tudor historians keen to make moral points about their own royal family, Richard had been the necessary evil required to bring about the final purge to heal a sick society.

Over his career, Shakespeare wrote nine plays about the Plantagenets – their titles name the Yorkist and Lancastrian rivals who fought for the crown. *Richard II* was deposed by Bolingbroke, who became *Henry IV*, whose son *Henry V* died young, leaving the throne to his child, the mentally weak *Henry VI*. *Richard III*, the next play in historical sequence, stands alone but Shakespeare's audiences would have seen and 'read' it imaginatively as the culmination of a great sweep of troubled English history dramatised in the three parts of *Henry VI*, written immediately before it.

You don't have to study the Henry plays, but you should know that *Richard III*'s pattern of cursing and divine retribution grows directly from their subject matter. One example illustrates the point – in *Henry VI Part 1*, Joan of Arc curses Richard's father in words that resonate with the sun imagery that opens and closes *Richard III*. She says: 'May never glorious sun reflex his beams/Upon the country where you make abode;/But darkness and the gloomy shade of death/Environ you' (1HenVI, V.4.87–90).

Shakespeare's Richard

One of Shakespeare's main sources is Edward Hall's *The Union of the Noble and Illustre Famelies of Lancastre and York* (1548), mostly because it copies the very negative description of a 'crook-backed, malicious, deep dissimulator' from Thomas More's *History of King Richard the Third* (1557).

More could have had no direct knowledge of Richard (he was only about seven in 1485) but he grew up in the household of Cardinal Morton. In Shakespeare's play, Morton is still only Bishop of Ely: he trots off to fetch strawberries for Richard at a crucial moment (III.4.34). We find out later that Morton has joined Richmond (IV.3.46).

Hall also copied material from the Tudor court historian Polydore Vergil's *Anglicae Historiae* (1534, with many later editions). Vergil was commissioned by Henry VII (Richmond) specifically to establish Richard III's bad reputation. This is an interesting example of 'spin', Tudor-style, to manufacture a dead monster.

Q Read Richard's villainy speeches from *3Henry VI*, III.2.124–95 and V.6.68–93. Actors often incorporate these lines into the first soliloquy in *Richard III*; watch Olivier's film version to hear most of the lines.

Shakespeare's Queen Margaret

Five years after Henry VI's funeral in 1471, his widow Queen Margaret left England for France, where she died in 1482.

Shakespeare re-creates her as a still-living character who 'haunts' Edward's and Richard's palace, dishing out curses and prophecies to those who remain alive at the end of the York and Lancaster wars. No-one is spared because all (even children) share the taint of dynastic blood-guilt. Margaret fits in with the play's scheme of retributive justice, playing a role like Nemesis (sometimes called Fate), the Greek goddess who measured out misery and happiness to mortals and administered punishment for crimes.

Actors and Richard

Shakespeare's larger-than-life character has always been a magnet for actors. Find Scott Colley's *Richard's Himself Again: A Stage History of Richard III* to read about some famous Richards. Modern actors like to share their experience of encountering Richard imaginatively. Find Anthony Sher's published diary and rehearsal record *Year of the King* (1985), Al Pacino's film essay *Looking for Richard* (1996) and Ian McKellen's annotated screenplay (1996), all of which document the challenging process of bringing Shakespeare's most popular villain to life for new audiences. (See References & Reading for publication details.)

Notes on dukes, cousins and boars

Shakespeare's history plays are full of subtle information about status, clan rivalry, wealth, political power and regional family pride. These references would have been common knowledge to the original audiences, but can be difficult for us to follow, especially when 'Derby' in one scene is 'Stanley' in another, and uncles speak of nephews as cousins.

Close adult relatives in Shakespeare's plays address each other affectionately as 'cousin' (or 'coz' sometimes), whether they really are cousins (like Richard and Buckingham), or a grandparent speaking to grandchildren (Duchess of York to Clarence's children), or uncle (Richard) talking to nephews.

It is easier to understand the characters and their titles if you know that British peerage has five ranks of nobility after the monarch and royal children (prince, princess). Highest in rank is Duke (e.g. York, Gloucester, Clarence, Buckingham), then Marquis (e.g. Dorset), Earl (e.g. Rivers, Derby, Richmond), Viscount and lastly Baron/Baronet. Most are entitled to be addressed as 'Lord'. After that, it's knights (e.g. Sir William Catesby) and gentlemen – then the common folk like us.

Richard is given his Dukedom of Gloucester by his brother the king. People can inherit titles or collect them as rewards. Buckingham anticipates Richard's gift of the Earldom of Hereford (which will give him land, property and revenue). The Earl of Derby is also known as Lord Stanley (his family surname, used often by Richard to be less polite than giving him his higher-ranked title).

Family allegiances on the battlefield were identified in the Middle Ages by heraldic symbols on shields, banners and clothes. The first 'College of Heralds' was established in London in 1484 by Richard III's royal charter – its purpose was to keep records of coats of arms and devise new ones. Shakespeare works Richard's York family symbol, the *White Rose en Soleil* (with the sun's rays flaring out from behind the rose) into a dramatic metaphor of Richard's rising and setting fortunes. Derby's prophetic dream (III.2) takes Richard's personal heraldic 'badge', a tusked white boar (signifying courage), and turns it into a monstrous supernatural threat.

GENRE, STRUCTURE & STYLE

Genre

Richard III combines several generic forms to develop themes and characters.

Tragic history

Aristotle's concept of *hamartia*, the hero's tragic 'flaw', helps us understand the complex central character. Richard's historical reputation gave Shakespeare the basic ideas to form a diabolical but attractive monster as Richard rises, and a pitiable flawed human as he falls by divine will.

Aristotelian ideas about the tragic fall from greatness informed a genre known as *'de casibus'* literature ('about the fall of ...'), which was popular well before Shakespeare's time. Such stories reminded Christians about the catastrophic fall of the angel Lucifer from heaven to hell for aspiring to be like God; the deadly sin of pride is a common cause of human downfall in this genre.

History is full of examples of the fall of great ones through ambition. The Wars of the Roses gave an anonymous author of *A Mirror for Magistrates* (1559) plenty of subject matter for an Elizabethan *de casibus* collection, including moralised accounts of the tragic falls of Richard, Duke of York, Henry VI, Clarence, Hastings, Buckingham and Jane Shore.

Two references in *Richard III* illustrate the tragic focus. In I.3, Queen Margaret warns Dorset not to insult her until he's known grief like hers: 'They that stand high have many blasts to shake them/And if they fall, they dash themselves to pieces' (I.3.258–9). And, almost at the end of the play, Buckingham's ghost makes it clear that 'God and good angels fight on Richmond's side', while 'Richard falls in height of all his *pride*' (V.3.176–7, my emphasis).

An anonymous play *The True Tragedy of Richard III* (published in 1594) combines Senecan revenge drama and English history. Shakespeare knew this play (he quotes from it in *Hamlet*), and adds divine retribution for sin, the basis of popular morality drama, to the generic mix.

Senecan tragedy

This genre is named after the Roman playwright, moralist and tutor to Emperor Nero. Seneca followed the tradition of Greek tragedy and sensationalised it for Roman tastes. Senecan features in *Richard III* include blood and violence onstage, heavy moralising, vengeful ghosts, weeping over corpses, warnings through omens and prophecies, dreams of horrors waiting for guilty souls in the underworld, and a sense of an inevitable tragic fate.

Morality drama

Medieval plays with biblical subjects continued to be performed into the sixteenth century, but shared their dramatic space with another more contemporary kind of theatre, the 'morality play'. This theatrical form dramatised theological issues in contemporary human life, using lively personifications to identify human and spiritual qualities.

The best-known morality play, still performed today, is *Everyman* (written around 1490). Its central character represents all people: he carelessly wanders through life enjoying good times with his mate 'Fellowship'. Just when he is most assured of life, Death turns up to summon his soul to God's judgement. The rest of the play shows Everyman desperately trying to find companions to accompany him on his last journey, while things that gave value to his earthly life (wealth, beauty, strength – and fellowship) desert him. Only his 'Good Deeds' is willing to accompany him and speak for his soul. There are touches of humour as cowardly mates slink away with silly excuses, but the overall message of *Everyman* is serious – examine your conscience and sort out the state of your soul, because death can come at any time.

Richard III is indebted to plays like *Everyman* for thematic concerns with the power of conscience, an awareness of life's fragility, and the concept of a divine 'All-seer' taking note of human activity.

Tudor Interludes with the Vice

Think of an early sixteenth-century Interlude as a shortened comic version of a morality play, with named types such as 'Mercy', 'Mankind' and 'Wisdom' sharing the stage with characters such as 'Mischief', 'Nought', 'Idleness' and 'Iniquity'. The last four are known as Vices – and Richard III tells us he's behaving 'like the formal Vice Iniquity' in a quick-witted moment (III.1.82).

The Vice is a tempter figure, personifying all Seven Deadly Sins (wrath, pride, sloth, envy, lust, gluttony and avarice). His dramatic purpose is to entertain, dialoguing with the audience, encouraging characters to indulge themselves and commit sins with him. He collects souls for hell, instigates cruel fun and controls dramatic events until moral order is restored at the end.

Richard III has several traces of the Interlude's comic mayhem:

- Lady Anne constantly refers to Richard as a devil – 'fiend', 'minister of hell', 'foul devil' (I.2). At the successful conclusion to his wooing scene, he claims that his only help came from 'the plain devil and dissembling looks' (I.2.237).
- Although often called a devil, the Vice is more of a soul-gathering agent. This is exactly how Margaret describes Richard: 'hell's black intelligencer;/Only reserved their factor to buy souls/And send them thither' (IV.4.71–3).

- Notice many examples of grotesque comedy with violence, e.g. in the scene of Clarence's 're-christening' prefaced by his murderers debating 'conscience' and punning on making 'a sop' of their victim (I.4). Any scene where Richard is fooling someone has the same unsettling mixture, with violence just under the surface.
- At the end of an Interlude, the Vice is punished by being carried off to hell or hanged. His defeat restores moral order. If Richmond's character seems undeveloped, consider that in a morality scheme he is only required onstage briefly to represent Richard's opposite (angel against devil, good king against bad tyrant) and restore peace.

Structure

Richard III is a long play (twenty-five scenes in five acts) with over fifty speaking parts. It is dominated by the voices of Richard, Buckingham and Margaret, with memorable set-piece speeches from individuals such as Hastings and Richmond. The lamenting women's scenes function as an extended commentary.

Narrative development is in two huge movements:

- **Acts I to III** are energised by Richard's single-minded drive towards the crown. They are fast-paced and rich in details about the past that has formed the present. Murders and curses set up revenge expectations, even though Richard seems unstoppable. His wit and engagement with the audience are evident.
- In **Act IV** tragic reversals of fortune begin for Buckingham and then Richard. **Act V** demonstrates how divine retribution replaces individual revenge-taking. Curses and their fulfilment shape the dramatic pattern that focuses on moral questions of guilt, conscience and deception revealed. Richard relates less to the audience and his wit becomes bitter.

Use of repetition

Patterns of repetition in the play are building blocks for dramatic action and thematic development; they connect and explore key ideas.

An example of repetition is paired scenes, such as Richard's two wooings – the first of Anne (I.2), which succeeds; and the second of Elizabeth (IV.4), which fails. They illustrate the playing out of core moral values, the idea that 'as you sow, so shall you reap' – bad decisions will come back to haunt you.

Style

Shakespeare's choice of blank verse (in iambic pentameter, with five stresses per line) or prose (e.g. for Clarence's debating murderers) signals whether scenes are to be understood as intimate or formal, serious or comic.

Note the following key elements of style:

- **Slower rhythms** of reflective speeches, and shared or echoed viewpoints as people meditate, grieve and compare woes – for example, women are 'alone together', lost in their private sorrows but echoing each other.
- **Stichomythia** – quick exchanges back and forth – when Richard is closely engaged in argument (e.g. I.2.109–14).
- **Dramatic irony** – where we know something a character doesn't. This affects how we hear what they are saying in their ignorance (e.g. Hastings). The effect is intensified when other characters are 'in the know' (like Buckingham), further isolating the victim.

Refer to Moseley's *Richard III Penguin Critical Studies* (1989), Chapter 9, 'Language, Style and Rhetoric' (pp.101–9) for a more detailed discussion of stylistic features.

Q How does the sun and weather imagery track the rise and set of the House of York's fortunes, and suggest the general 'climate' of the times?

SCENE-BY-SCENE ANALYSIS

Line numbers in brackets at the beginnings of paragraphs refer to steps in dramatic development, often related to character entrances and exits. All line references are to the Penguin edition.

Act 1

I.1 Summary: *A long war between York and Lancaster is over. Richard Duke of Gloucester explains his ambition to seize the crown from his brother Edward, who is terminally ill. He plans to eliminate opposition from his brother Clarence and to marry Lady Anne, the widow of a man he murdered.*

This scene has four dramatic movements. By the end we have discovered much about Richard's character.

(1–41: key soliloquy) Richard's 'Now is the winter ...' revealing his inner thoughts to the audience is one of the best-known opening speeches in English drama. Notice how his argument develops, each point revealing deeply hidden motivations. He explains the dramatic situation, indicating what he hopes will further his plan to seize the crown. Because he shares his deepest feelings so honestly, we are drawn strongly towards him, even though his character is obviously devious and malignant.

(42–120) Richard meets his brother, George, Duke of Clarence immediately after telling us that he's plotting Clarence's death. 'What means this armèd guard ...?' (42) is ironic – Richard knows it means he's succeeded in casting suspicion of treason on his brother. His insincere joke about 'new-christening' George in the Tower (50) makes light of the danger George faces. They share misogynistic bawdy talk about Edward's mistress, Jane Shore.

(121–42) As Clarence goes to the Tower, Lord Hastings is released. Richard's brief conversation with Hastings about Edward's illness alerts us to the prospect that there will be more victims.

(143–62) Richard discloses his plan to marry 'Warwick's youngest daughter', Lady Anne, the widow of Edward, Prince of Wales and daughter-in-law of the Lancastrian king Henry VI. Richard killed both men – so Anne is hardly likely to want their murderer as a husband ... is she?

Q Is Richard's view that he is unlovable because of his deformity designed to awaken the audience's sympathy? If so, does it work?

Q How does Richard's manipulation of double meanings in conversation deceive his victims into believing he's on their side – while also demonstrating his clever duplicity to us?

I.2 Summary: *Richard intercepts Lady Anne as she accompanies the body of her father-in-law King Henry VI to burial. In a brilliant 'wooing scene' Richard turns her grieving hatred of him to acceptance of marriage.*

(1–32) Anne relates the historical circumstances behind this moment. She articulates the first of several curses, targeting Richard and any future child and wife of his (14–30). By the end of the scene her curse rebounds as she becomes Richard's wife (dramatic irony).

(33–114) Disharmony between the couple is signalled in tight oppositional language (devil/angel etc.) and fast-paced dialogue. Anne demonstrates Richard's incontrovertible guilt in public because the king's

dead body bleeds when its murderer is nearby. They play an escalating game of insult and justification (68–124) until Richard's shockingly direct sexual suggestion about being in her bed ends the first match of wits.

Lines become shared (109–14), a sure sign that there is intense emotional connection – positive or negative – between speakers. This stichomythia (quick succession of verbal exchanges in single lines) winds up the tension towards a climax.

(115–83) Richard shifts the blame for his crimes onto her ('Your beauty was the cause', 121) and then invites her to end his suffering for love (her fault again) by killing him. When she refuses to be his 'executioner' he presents an apparent choice of alternatives. In fact, she is not bound to choose either – she knows he's a 'dissembler' so why isn't she thinking?

(184–226) Anne's last feeble attempt to repel Richard's verbal onslaught suggests her exhaustion. The stichomythia heightens tension not to a climax but to capitulation as Richard places a ring on her hand.

Key point

You have an editorial stage direction: 'She puts on the ring' (after line 202). Think about this from an actor's point of view. In most productions, Richard physically slips the ring on her finger, while she no longer resists but passively signals her unwillingness to share the betrothal which the ring symbolises. Nothing in the text so far suggests that she could be so directly complicit as to perform this action herself, and her line (202) reinforces this sense. Most actors playing Richard try to make the 'ring' moment as repulsively seductive as possible, with Anne looking stunned.

(227–63) Richard's exulting soliloquy is designed to swing us from sympathetic pity to shocked admiration for an unexpected sexual triumph. He plans to reward himself with some new clothes (fashion was the Vice's weakness; see 'Tudor Interludes with the Vice' in the Genre section).

Q How do the words and rhythms in the dialogue of I.2 suggest specific choreography and non-verbal interactions between Richard and Anne?

Q Why does Anne succumb to Richard? At what points can you hear the change in the conversation?

I.3 Summary: *Queen Elizabeth's family wait anxiously for news of the King's health. Richard stirs up their enmities and anxieties. Queen Margaret, waiting for revenge, curses several individuals.*

This scene illustrates how Edward's brothers and other hereditary peers (especially the powerful Duke of Buckingham) hate Elizabeth, her commoner brother (Earl Rivers) and her sons (Marquess of Dorset and Lord Grey) by a previous marriage, all now made 'noblemen' by her royal second husband.

(1–41) When Edward dies, Queen Elizabeth fears her family will be destroyed and her two young sons by Edward will be endangered – although they are heirs to the throne, their uncle Richard is their nominated Protector.

(42–109) Richard delays his entrance for maximum theatrical effect: his verbal attack darkens the mood. His ploy is to stir up more discord and anxiety with his pretence of 'righteous' anger at supposed mischief-making.

(110–56) A significant character enters the scene – Queen Margaret, the embittered old widow of Henry VI. Pay attention to her asides: because she comments grimly on each of Richard's points about his loyal service to Edward, she effectively reminds us that even his honourable actions have been tainted with blood.

Key scene: Margaret's curses

(157–302) Queen Margaret steps out of her hiding place to confront everyone as rebels and thieves. They treat her behaviour and words as a mad joke. However, she curses or predicts a deadly end for each of her mockers (187–213 and 216+), and every word she utters comes true.

(305–18) After a convincing show of hypocrisy for the departing crowd, Richard delivers a revealing short soliloquy on his skill (323–37) before moving on to arrange Clarence's murder.

I.4 Summary: *In prison, Clarence describes his nightmare of drowning and his soul going to punishment in the underworld; two murderers, after a brief black comic debate, carry out Richard's orders and kill him.*

(2–63) Clarence's horrific nightmare is about to happen in reality. His troubled conscience gives rise to a 'tempest' in his sinful soul (66–74). His afterlife glimpse of hellish punishment combines Classical (ancient Greek and Roman) and Christian imagery.

(101–63) The murderers forget Richard's warning about Clarence's power to plead (I.3.345–8), giving him time to argue his innocence (even though he's just confessed his guilt). Clarence makes a strong moral point

about murder as breaking God's commandments (198–200), only to have it turned against him (204–13). Note the irony when Clarence tries to defend his sinful actions as brotherly. His last pleas turn the Second Murderer to pity and repentance – too late.

Note that, although the Penguin edition identifies two characters as 'Keeper' and 'Brackenbury' in I.4, most editions combine the two: in performance they are always played as one and the same. This adds poignancy to Brackenbury's short speech on the cares of princes (a favourite Elizabethan meditation), and makes his 'guiltless' response to Clarence's murderers appear both spineless and politically astute – he understands that Clarence is a 'problem' that needs solving.

Shakespeare's audience would have recognised an echo of the 'bad' and 'good' thieves crucified on either side of Jesus. The 'good' thief repents and his soul is saved, but the 'bad' refuses and is damned. While Clarence is certainly not Christ-like, his pleas for lawful justice are fair. The religious parallel is reinforced by the Second Murderer's reference to Pontius Pilate's famous hand-washing (I.4.275).

Q Brackenbury senses the reason why two ruffians want to see Clarence but declines to get involved (92–8). Is he doing the right thing?

Q Why do the murderers have a long 'debate' scene (like a morality play) before deciding to act? What can an audience learn from this?

By the end of Act I …

Richard has brought about Clarence's death and has won Anne as his wife.

Act II

II.1 Summary: *King Edward appears to have reconciled the Queen's family with Hastings and Buckingham. Richard's news of Clarence's execution causes Edward to collapse, and anxious bickering returns. Richard and Buckingham become allies.*

(1–44) Edward's superficial peace-making is signalled by showy kisses and handshaking. Buckingham makes an over-elaborate oath of loyalty to Queen Elizabeth (32–40). Does he mean it honestly? Look ahead to his speech at II.2.146–50 and actions in III.7. We imagine the consequences if this oath should rebound on him – as it does in IV.2 and V.1.

(47–96) Richard again delays his entrance for dramatic effect. He hypocritically enhances everyone's peaceful mood before using Elizabeth's innocent suggestion about Clarence to drop his bombshell – Clarence is dead … on the King's orders.

Q How does Richard make Edward accept responsibility for Clarence's death?

II.2 Summary: *Royal women gather to grieve for Edward and express fears about Richard's plans.*

(1–33) The Duchess of York warns her grandson not to trust (his uncle) Gloucester's show of affection. The boy's mistaken belief in the sincerity of Richard's weeping echoes his father Clarence's description to his murderers of Richard's brotherly sobs (I.4.247–9). This demonstrates how convincingly Richard can fake emotional closeness.

(34–100) Queen Elizabeth's grief draws unsympathetic complaints from Clarence's children and shared grief from the Duchess. Notice parallels and repetitions – we realise this is a consequence of family bitterness carrying over generations. Elizabeth's family members stress the need to retain power by claiming the crown for the child Prince Edward.

(101–45) Richard leaves Buckingham to suggest delicate arrangements for getting Prince Edward from Ludlow to London for coronation without upsetting the family. The women's fears are calmed by Richard's affability – they don't think he's manipulating the situation ...

(146–54) ... neither does Buckingham: Richard says he'll be guided 'as a child' (153). This short but significant dialogue reveals Buckingham's duplicity – remember his oath to support Elizabeth's family in the previous scene.

Q Why does the Duchess not tell Clarence's children about their father's death?

II.3 Summary: *Chorus-like citizens mirror anxiety about disruption to the state if the King is dead and the heir is a child.*

This scene evokes the tone of a Chorus in Greek tragedy, producing a distancing effect. Notice how the citizens represent shades of opinion: the First expresses optimism; the Second is fearful but puts faith in the government; the Third senses danger.

Q What specific anxieties preoccupy the citizens?

II.4 Summary: *Royal women wait with Archbishop for Prince Edward to arrive in London. His little brother, Richard (Duke of York), talks with grandmother about Richard as a boy. Queen Elizabeth's fears are realised – relatives have been arrested and will be executed at Pomfret.*

(1–37) Notice the sense of anxiety in the women: they have no protection now King Edward is dead. The bright child York, close to his uncle, has heard negative rumours about Richard: his cautious mother warns him to guard his tongue since spies could be listening – 'Pitchers have ears' (37; note that jug handles were called 'lugs').

(38–73) News of family arrests at Pomfret leads Elizabeth to foresee tyranny; the Duchess sees that the family war for possession of the crown will recommence. Elizabeth hopes that religious sanctuary will be a safe place for them, something Richard wouldn't dare to violate.

Q How does Richard's mother's information about him reveal her feelings?

By the end of Act II …

Richard has permanently disrupted Edward's family peace, hastened the King's death and cleared away the Queen's relatives so that he is the Protector of the royal children.

Act III

III.1 Summary: *Richard and Buckingham welcome Prince Edward. Buckingham's 'sensible' argument releases little brother York from his mother's protection. Richard promises to reward Buckingham with the earldom of Hereford.*

(1–60) Richard cleverly allows Buckingham to 'take charge' of a tricky political and religious situation in breaking sanctuary to unite the Princes. Their mother Elizabeth can't blame Richard for this act of sacrilege; furthermore, she still trusts Buckingham. Richard makes Buckingham feel confident that an earldom is his for the asking – a dangerous assumption, as he'll discover in IV.2.

(61–94) This brief but significant exchange about the origins of the Tower and Julius Caesar introduces broader ideas about how 'truth' and 'fame' are remembered through history. (See 'History and memory' in the Themes, Ideas & Values section.)

(95–150) The children pass from the stage into historical speculation and popular legend. Historically 'the Princes in the Tower' disappeared from public view when Richard III became king, while rumours of their murder spread.

Richard adopts the role of a wise, protective, amusing uncle. Hear the double meaning of 'my thoughts' sovereign' to Edward (2; i.e. you're the king who's foremost in my thoughts as my rival), and his sinister asides about the boy's smartness and noble aspirations.

Richard's dagger reminds us of the Vice's wooden dagger. We are meant to appreciate a double meaning of 'with all my heart' (111; i.e. 'I really want to stick my dagger into you'), and the jeering sexual innuendo of the child having a man's 'weapon'. York's expression 'like an ape' (130) draws attention to Richard's hunchback as an object of ridicule.

Q How does Shakespeare characterise the Princes as individuals and suggest an age difference?

Q Does Edward sound as though he would make a good king?

III.2 Summary: *Lord Hastings rejects Stanley's dream warning about Richard. Hastings will be Richard's next victim, brought down by being too confident that he's secure.*

This scene is full of dramatic irony. Although he has no reason to suspect that Richard, who greeted him so warmly in I.1, would target him now, Hastings expresses a foolish pride and unconcern for others' deaths. We know better what's in store, from the conversation about him between Richard, Buckingham and Catesby at the end of III.1.

(1–34) Hastings rejects the offer of escape from Derby (Lord Stanley), mocking his friend's prophetic dream to beware Richard, the heraldic boar. He is also unconcerned at the suspiciously divided council meetings set to arrange Prince Edward's coronation because his 'good friend Catesby' (22) will keep them informed.

(35–71) Hastings speaks frankly to Catesby (already co-opted as Richard's spy). Note the irony in Hastings wishing himself beheaded rather than disloyal to the true heirs (43–4) – Catesby knows, as we do, which of these will in fact be the outcome (69–71).

(72–123) Hastings's foolish confidence is emphasised in four brief conversations as he sets out for the Tower meeting:

- with the anxious Derby, whose views on life's uncertainty should make Hastings pause to think
- with Pursuivant Hastings (i.e. 'follower', a herald) – Hastings boasts and pays him to celebrate the enemies' executions with a drink
- with priest 'Sir John' – Hastings cheerfully promises to pay him next Sunday
- with friendly Buckingham, who makes an ironic joke about not needing a priest. Buckingham's sinister aside predicts Hastings's death in the Tower rather than dinner (20–1).

Q How would you describe Hastings and Derby's friendship from the evidence of this scene?

III.3 Summary: *Rivers, Grey and Vaughan executed.*

The scene begins with a reference to the ominous history of Pomfret (Pontefract) Castle, where Richard II, another deposed king, was murdered. The executions are supervised by Richard's loyal follower Ratcliffe, who speaks 'hurry up' lines recalling Death's words from *Everyman*.

The victims give a Chorus-like recapitulation of Margaret's curse on them, and remind the audience who remain on her list (Richard, Buckingham and Hastings) with vengeful hopes that God will answer her full curse.

Q How does this scene prepare us for the fall of Hastings in the next one?

III.4 Summary: *Richard's dangerous nature revealed in Hastings's sudden execution.*

(1–20) Buckingham sets a trap, leading Hastings to speak confidently for the absent Richard, at which moment …

(21–58) … Richard's delayed entrance breaks up the council meeting. His exaggerated banter baits the trap for Hastings, who senses too late that something's wrong after Richard and Buckingham leave again (48–57).

(59–79) Richard returns to spring the trap, creating an instant mood change. Hastings is nervous and too quick to condemn perpetrators (63–6) when Richard makes 'witchcraft' accusations against the Queen and Jane Shore (now Hastings's mistress).

(80–107) Hastings is isolated as 'friends' flee the room. He goes to his execution grieving for England's fate under Richard's rule and

moralising about the uncertainty of life (echoing Clarence's sea/drowning imagery in I.4).

Q At what point does Hastings guess he is Richard's target?

III.5 Summary: *Pretending they've discovered Hastings's treason, Richard and Buckingham persuade the Lord Mayor to accept their 'national security' reasons for his unwitnessed execution without trial. Next step – illegitimacy of King Edward to be rumoured.*

This scene is a prelude to III.7, Richard's elaborately staged confidence trick, stage-managed by Buckingham. We are meant to appreciate their cunning enjoyment of this dangerous political gamble with a big pay-off.

(1–11) Richard and Buckingham discuss, then demonstrate, their play-acting skills. Their special costumes (old armour) suggest to the gullible Mayor how hastily they had to prepare to 'fight' against the suddenly revealed assassination plot of the 'traitor' Hastings. Buckingham boasts he knows how to appear distraught, like a professional tragedian, in voice tone, facial expression and gestures.

(12–70) Richard makes a 'lamenting' speech over their ghastly stage prop, dead Hastings's head, implicating Mistress Shore in her lover's fall. Buckingham gives a 'regretful' speech that Hastings was beheaded by well-meaning loyalists before the Mayor could be called to hear his confession and so be able to justify the execution to sceptical citizens – this is the main point of the charade. The Mayor appears convinced: 'your grace's word shall serve' (61).

(71–101) With his reward in mind (see III.1) and forgetful of his promise of loyalty to Edward's queen and children (I.1.33–40), Buckingham enthusiastically agrees to 'play the orator' (94) and spread slanders about Edward and his sons. He is confident he can swing public opinion to choose Richard as king.

(102–8) Richard's brief sinister soliloquy about his plans for the royal children changes the dramatic mood from horrible fun to serious anticipation of cruelty.

Q Why is Buckingham and Richard's 'performance' deliberately 'over the top'?

Q Trace Margaret's curses and how they have been realised up to this point. Are there any clues as to who will be next?

III.6 Summary: *Chorus-like Scrivener reveals injustice of Hastings's execution.*

The legal clerk reflects that he was asked to write a document against Hastings at least six hours before Richard made his accusation (III.4). He's afraid to be a whistle-blower but knows Richard's procedure was illegal, enabled by a 'palpable device' – that is, this written legal indictment generated to prosecute and authorise punishment for an unproven crime.

Q Is he speaking directly to us? What difference does it make?

III.7 Summary: *At Baynard's Castle (Richard's London home on the Thames), Richard and Buckingham play their 'holy show' until people reluctantly accept Richard as king.*

(1–43) Buckingham is shocked that the citizens have resisted his brilliant persuasion, and Richard expresses contempt for the citizens' daring to frustrate his plans. This dialogue would have aroused unsympathetic feelings in Shakespeare's London audiences, who were proud of their municipal institutions and freedoms.

(44–54) Buckingham enjoys directing Richard on how to stage a hypocritical 'big scene' in another attempt to win the citizens' approval. The prayer book is an essential 'stage prop' here, and note the careful positioning of Richard above the crowd (under the metal roofing 'leads', 54).

Key point

Buckingham uses a clever musical analogy of 'ground' and 'descant' for this drama. Richard posed 'between two churchmen' gives people a basic visual idea of his holiness, like a 'ground' in music (a basic repeated pattern of notes). Buckingham will elaborate on Richard's virtue, like a descant line (which decorates the basic pattern). Richard uses a similar musical image in I.1: envious of the 'delight' in the 'weak piping' music of sunny peace, he suggests that all he can make is an out-of-tune 'descant' on his misshapen shadow.

(94–221) Richard makes a dramatic entrance above the crowd. Notice how rehearsed and artificial the duologue between Richard and Buckingham is, a long moral 'debate' leading to Richard's two refusals (153+, 206) and then Buckingham's supposedly angry exit with the crowd (219). Then Catesby's precisely timed ringing plea from the roof calls everyone back.

(222–46) A *coup de théâtre* for Richard, playing the timid holy innocent reluctant to take the crown (playing the 'maid's part', 50). Everything he says is contrary to what he's told us he actually thinks and desires.

Q How do Buckingham and Catesby collaborate to 'warm up' the Mayor and the crowd (55–93)?

Q What makes the crowd resistant?

By the end of Act III …

Richard has achieved the crown – King Richard's fall begins immediately in Act IV.

Act IV

IV.1 Summary: *Royal women prevented from visiting the Princes by Protector/King's orders. Lady Anne summoned to Westminster to be crowned Queen. Queen Elizabeth urges her son Dorset to escape overseas to Earl of Richmond. Women lament, ending with prayer for the Princes.*

The presence of Derby is significant – he is Richmond's stepfather. An example of coping with divided loyalties, he is obedient to King Richard but also helpful to Dorset.

Notice the sad dramatic power in Elizabeth's prayer to the Tower for the Princes (98–103). There is a terrible irony in the mother asking stones to pity children – when their living uncle will not. This prayer enhances the cruel effect of the next two scenes.

Key point

The royal women think of themselves as being cursed and perpetually burdened with grief. Elizabeth knows her name is 'ominous to children' (40); Richard's mother curses her own womb for bearing him. When she displaces Elizabeth as Queen, Anne reminds women of her own rebounding curse for not resisting Richard (see I.2).

Q Anne is another reluctant queen, but is the joylessness of her position partly her own fault?

IV.2 Summary: *Richard crowned king; rift with Buckingham; plans to kill Princes in the Tower and then Queen Anne. Richard begins to think about Richmond.*

(1–4) Richard makes Buckingham support him physically as he takes his seat on the throne – a brief but calculated exercise of power. The split third line shows that these movements take significant time onstage, a public demonstration of Richard's authority.

What should be a high point for Richard is ironically the beginning of his anxiety. His character change begins, from the wickedly funny Vice to an insecure paranoid tyrant. The scene reveals areas of vulnerability that Richard needs to address.

How to consolidate status as king?

- *(5–31)* Richard's apparently casual questions lead to irritated wordplay on 'True, noble prince' (15–16), as Buckingham appears 'dull' (17) to suggestion about killing Prince Edward.
- *(65–81)* Richard arranges the Princes' murder with Tyrrel.
- *(49–64)* Richard plans to marry his niece, Princess Elizabeth, after killing Anne and disposing of Clarence's children (other potential challengers) – even loyal Catesby is surprised by Richard's speed (55).

How to deal with opposition?

- *(46–8)* Stanley's news that Richmond is attracting important refugees activates an obsessive thought in Richard's mind – what can he do?
- *(82–121)* Buckingham becomes an irritation. Between leaving the stage (26) and returning to claim his reward, Richard has discarded him.

Buckingham knows he is in danger after Richard's outburst (111), remembering Hastings whose sense of security he mocked (III.2). He repeatedly tries to gain Richard's attention while Richard addresses the taciturn Stanley (82–117). Tension builds (stichomythia in shared lines) with Richard's apparently unrelated enquiry about time.

(94–106) Richard recalls prophecies about Richmond, reflecting his changing personality: he begins to believe the kind of superstitious predictions he previously scorned – or made up himself to do mischief.

Q What signs can you identify of a shift in Richard's character from Vice-like energy to human awareness?

IV.3 Summary: *Tyrrel describes the Princes' murder.*

(1–22) Like the Messenger in a Greek tragedy, Tyrrel reports violence committed by Dighton and Forrest offstage in a short emotional soliloquy. He conveys the enormity of this deed and acknowledges the villains' 'conscience and remorse' (20).

Key point

We're given time to pause and reflect on the murder of children, the royal heirs, recalling Richard's lack of 'Tear-falling pity' (IV.2.64) even though the murderers themselves are left speechless.

(36–43) Richard's upsurge of optimism in this grim 'stock-taking' soliloquy briefly reasserts his 'Vice' personality. His impetus to become a 'jolly thriving wooer' (43) is ironically diverted by news of military threats from Richmond and Buckingham. Compare this to Richard's thoughts in his opening soliloquy (I.1), when soldier Richard reminisced about war and had no use for peace because he couldn't be a lover.

Q Does Tyrrel's report of the Princes' murder affect us more strongly than other executions in the play?

Q Why does Richard regain his energy once he realises he'll have to fight to keep the crown?

IV.4 Summary: *Royal women focus on Richard. After being cursed by his mother, Richard pressures Elizabeth to let him marry her daughter, his niece.*

(1–8) Queen Margaret's 'dire induction', like a ghostly avenger observing the action, sets the scene's tone – the time is ripe for divine retribution. Note her vivid image of Death waiting open-mouthed to devour 'mellow' fruit (all her enemies).

(9–134) Queen Elizabeth and the Duchess of York (Richard's mother) lament while Margaret (in asides) keeps a tally of revenge accomplished. Margaret refocuses passive grief into active cursing against Richard (47–58) and instructs other women on how to curse. When she exits, Richard's mother takes up the attack (132 onwards).

(135–96) Richard makes a noisy military entrance. Notice how words (up to now his strongest weapon) catch him out, first in an 'intercept' exchange (136–7), then in a string of 'where …?' questions, which he evades by ordering 'clamorous report of war' (loud trumpets and drums).

(197–431) Richard embarks on a 'wooing scene' by proxy. There is a dramatic emphasis on his depravity in proposing to marry his brother's daughter after killing her siblings and relatives. This is achieved through Elizabeth's stunned response – 'What, thou?' (267) – and then a moment of silence, until Richard coolly finishes her line with a sardonic invitation to share in his decision: 'Even so. How think you of it?'

The intense duologue (200–417) moves through stages, using wordplay and rhythmic shifts similar to I.2. However, there are significant differences in Richard's approach this time. He gets to the point more quickly and is less inventive; he is pragmatic about striking a bargain and irritated by Elizabeth's memories: 'Look what is done cannot be now amended' (291).

Elizabeth blocks his attempts to swear an oath of honest intention (366–87), retorting that: 'God's wrong is most of all' (377). She forces him to utter his reckless oath: 'Myself myself confound' (399–405) which will rebound on him in battle.

Elizabeth resists because she's morally stronger than Anne and as cunning as Richard. She pretends to 'be tempted of the devil' (418) so that Richard is fooled into thinking he's won the argument. He misunderstands her ambiguity in 'Shall I forget myself to be myself?' (420, i.e. 'I'll have to forget that I was mother and queen until you destroyed my heirs and position, in order to be queen mother again if I accept your offer'). Look ahead to IV.5.7–8, to find out that Elizabeth has already promised her daughter to Richmond.

(432–538) Richard panics at news of Richmond's invasion – he feels that external events are slipping out of his control. A sense of human vulnerability creeps in with 'Is the King dead?' (470), and heightened anxiety about his security is conveyed by 'What heir of York is there alive but we?' (471).

Q Trace other 'harvest' imagery that expresses ideas similar to Margaret's 'mellow' fruit image.

Q Richard's mother utters a final death curse (184–96) to which Richard makes no reply – has she frightened him, or doesn't he care?

IV.5 Summary: *Derby sends message of support to Richmond but must protect his son, Richard's hostage. Elizabeth supports her daughter's marriage to Richmond. Richmond's supporters are marching on London to claim the crown.*

This scene reminds us that divine retribution is on the way, but individuals are still vulnerable – even though Richard is offstage for this and the next scene.

Act V

V.1 Summary: *Buckingham is executed, remembering Margaret's prophecy.*

Buckingham's death on All Souls' Day (2 November – a Christian celebration honouring good souls) is appropriate punishment for his fake goodness and self-serving treachery. Divine retribution comes as Margaret predicted (I.3) and as he wished on himself 'in jest' (in II.1.32–40).

The scene reinforces the idea that retributive justice is fair – God is not mocked. Buckingham's sins are real but a pale imitation of Richard's, making us wonder what *his* fate will be.

V.2 Summary: *Richmond greets his followers.*

Richmond appears onstage at last – speaking as his country's rescuer from Richard's 'yoke of tyranny' (2). He presents an ugly image of Richard as a 'foul swine' in the centre of the country, ruining 'summer' crops and devouring people.

Compare this imagery with Richard's opening soliloquy (I.1) set in 'glorious summer' and enjoying the Yorkist 'sun' victory. His usurpation of the throne has changed the season back to winter and the weather to ominous gloom – sun won't shine on his battle. Richmond sees a lovely natural sunset, and we understand it is Richard's Yorkist 'sunset' (V.3.19–21).

Q How does sun imagery throughout Act V shape our perceptions of what will happen to Richard and Richmond?

V.3 Summary: *The night before battle, two armies camp in Bosworth Field. Ghosts visit Richmond and Richard; Richard's nightmare leads to a temporary questioning of conscience. The leaders deliver battle orations to their armies.*

A long scene that compares two leaders in human and spiritual ways in a series of paired episodes. The staging emphasises comparisons with two tents at opposite sides of the stage, emblazoned with heraldic badges and flags. These symbolise the rival strands of a dynasty that has engaged in a prolonged civil war, which this battle will finally resolve.

Leaders establish camp

(1–18) Richard, a seasoned soldier with the larger army, outwardly expresses confidence to cheer his followers. There is, though, an uneasiness in his wondering where he will 'lie' tomorrow (7–8). Does he sound convinced that 'the King's name is a tower of strength' (12)? He throws himself into activity to avoid nervous thoughts.

(19–46) Richmond sees the sunset and makes plans – hoping for the support of his stepfather Lord Stanley. Blunt's 'God give you quiet rest tonight' (43) eases the tension.

(47–79) Richard has lost his characteristic 'cheer of mind' (74); to keep busy, he checks armour and troop loyalties, and gives a special warning to Stanley.

(80–118) Stanley confers his blessing on Richmond, yet warns he'll have to 'deceive the time' (93) in battle to protect his stepbrother.

Leaders experience dream visions

(119–77) Richard's eleven victims curse him and bless Richmond in formulaic repetitions. Souls have an interest in the battle's outcome because cosmic and physical worlds have been disturbed by Richard's tyranny. The ghosts soothe Richmond with dreams of a morally just victory, while reminding Richard's conscience of his guilt, cursing his soul with despair and predicting his death in battle. Buckingham's final line identifies Richard as a tragic figure – he's not a devil but a flawed man who will fall 'in height of all his pride' (177).

(178–207) Richard's conscience-driven *psychomachia* (battle in the soul) is a debate between the fearful, despairing man and the remorseless egocentric monster, incapable of love or pity.

Leaders' orations to soldiers

(238–71) Richmond's 'God and our good cause' speech sets out the ideal scenario of a justified war against 'a bloody tyrant and a homicide' (247). His strong measured appeal is intended to unite the army in the defence of England's kingdom, country and domestic life.

(315–42) Richard's speech as a 'warlike sovereign' (303) is powerful but aggressive. He appeals to traditional English macho fears, casting Richmond as an unmanly 'milksop' leading French 'scum' who will steal

men's land and rape the women. Instead of invoking God, Richard's message calls on men to forget their conscience and not care whether they go to heaven or hell (313–14). His tyrant's 'law' is that might makes right (312).

Key point

Richard is fatally mistaken to think that a 'selfsame heaven' looks down on Richmond (287–8): the scene's comparisons show how differently these leaders relate to, and are watched by, 'heaven'.

Both leaders appeal to St George, patron saint of England and dragon-killer. Surely Richard is carried away by his own rhetoric – he shouldn't be asking for dragon's anger (350–1). Perhaps he unconsciously prefers to identify with a doomed fierce creature over the soldier-saint, Richmond's choice?

Q How does Richmond's serious belief in God's power compare with Buckingham's realisation (too late) that he never took seriously 'That high All-seer which I dallied with' (V.1.20)?

Q Does Richard ever understand what a conscience is all about?

V.4 Summary: *Richard's horse killed in battle; he refuses to escape.*

Richard's self-reliance is related to his lack of concern about losing his life. He is also driven by an overwhelming urge to kill his rival, a desire that is so strong he'll trade away his kingdom for a new horse.

Q Does Richard display any admirable qualities? What makes his self-reliance deadly to him? How is his bravery misplaced?

Q Does Richard understand what it really means to be the ruler of a kingdom?

V.5 Summary: *Richard is killed by Richmond, who accepts the crown from Derby (Lord Stanley) to become Henry VII.*

Appropriately, Richmond's first word as victor is 'God'. His speech ends the play with a benign vision of family and country under a united royal house and its heirs (namely, for Shakespeare's audiences, Elizabeth I).

Q What qualities in Richmond's speech suggest he'll be a good ruler?

CHARACTERS & RELATIONSHIPS

Instead of trying to discuss every character in a long play with over fifty speaking roles, focus on Richard's dominant presence first, then explore his interactions with other groups of characters.

Key point

While Richard usually embodies the most extreme example of a characteristic – such as deceit or pride – be aware that all characters are shown to be tainted with the same defects and sins because the whole society is affected by the 'corruption of abusing times' (Buckingham's phrase, III.7.198). When you identify a quality in Richard, always look for someone else in the play who shares a similar characteristic.

Richard (Duke of Gloucester, King)

Key quotes

'I am determined to prove a villain' (I.1.30)
'O, full of danger is the Duke of Gloucester' (Third Citizen, II.3.27)
'One that hath ever been God's enemy' (Richmond, V.3.253)
'... the troubler of the poor world's peace' (Margaret, I.3.220)

Find more quotes to explore the range of Richard's complexity. Each scene gives him an opportunity to try out another role, play word games and exercise his 'subtle, false and treacherous' skills (I.1.37). Here we trace three interpretations of his character: as Vice, actor and tragic hero.

Richard playing the Vice

Key quotes

'I do the wrong, and first begin to brawl' (I.3.323)
'Sin, death, and hell have set their marks on him' (Margaret, I.3.292)

Like the Vice character in Tudor Interludes (see the notes on 'Tudor Interludes with Vice' under Genre), Richard stirs up trouble, encourages false expectations, incites others to commit sins – and enjoys it.

Untroubled about being a hypocrite, he preaches lessons about virtue to Anne and later to his nephew about the danger of judging by outward show (III.1.9–11).

A **key scene** is III.1. In a sinister echo of the Vice's antics with a wooden dagger, Richard offers to 'give' his nephew his dagger and repeats the same grim threat in a joke about his sword, with sexual innuendo about the child wanting a man's 'weapon'. Violence lurks beneath his joking 'love'.

Key point

While the traditional Vice, with his obvious name like 'Iniquity' or 'Mischief', personified the Seven Deadly Sins, Richard is a much more sophisticated figure. As the play progresses he displays increasingly human characteristics, which allows Shakespeare to explore deeper ideas about conscience, remorse and just punishment.

Richard as actor

Key quote

'And seem a saint, when most I play the devil' (I.3.337)

- Notice Richard's frequent use of words like 'seem' and 'playing', suggesting a theatrical performance. He finds a willing 'cast' in Catesby, Ratcliffe and especially Buckingham as second 'lead', to make his 'scenes' plausible.
- **Key scenes** include I.1 (playing the emotionally upset brother to fool Clarence), I.2 (playing the 'rejected lover' which recasts Anne as a 'cruel mistress'), III.4 (playing the 'bewitched innocent' to destroy Hastings), and III.5 (exchanging performance tips with Buckingham before the big charade of III.7 to fool the Mayor).
- His 'lover' role fails to convince Elizabeth in IV.4 – how have his acting skills declined?
- His most intense dramatic dialogue is with himself in *psychomachia* (V.3.183–204), where he confronts his own terrifying duplicity.

Richard as tragic monster/hero

Key quotes

'What do I fear? Myself? There's none else by.' (v. 3. 183)
'Fool, of thyself speak well. Fool, do not flatter.' (v. 3. 193)
'I shall despair. There is no creature loves me …' (v. 3. 201)

Key point

In the first three acts Richard plays the Vice-like ambitious schemer – then he achieves the crown, becoming more human as he declines.

Why is Richard both attractive and a monster? Because he is capable of suffering? Because others refer negatively to his body? Because he tries to resist his own conscience and fools himself? Because when he gets the crown he has no use for it, other than to defend his position of power?

Richard's feudal pride as a royal Duke and his misogynistic anxieties about women in a man's world, especially his soldier's world, are recognisable, ingrained characteristics of his aristocratic heritage. Notice his similarity to Shakespeare's later tragic monster/hero Macbeth, a capable, intelligent and brave man who destroys himself through ambition. Ian McKellen based his interpretation of Richard on the idea of 'a soldier who has conquered his incapacities' but has nothing to do when the war's over (see McKellen's introduction to the screenplay for Loncraine's 1995 film, p.29).

What makes Richard's power politics 'evil' as opposed to cruel but expedient? In *3Henry VI*, III.2, he claims he can teach the 'murderous Machiavel' a few things – alerting prejudiced Elizabethan audiences to associate him with the Italian arch-villain. Machiavelli's well-known advice was that a ruler has to be prepared to act ruthlessly to preserve power (Niccolò Machiavelli, *Il principe (The Prince)*, 1513). See notes on 'Power' in the Themes, Ideas & Values section below.

Richard and his brothers

King Edward IV

Key quotes

'The King is sickly, weak, and melancholy' (Hastings, I.1.136)
'And more in peace my soul shall part to heaven,
Since I have made my friends at peace on earth.' (II.1.5–6)
'O God! I fear thy justice will take hold
On me and you, and mine and yours, for this' (II.1.133–4)

Edward's dying hope is to use his royal power as God's representative to make peace between the aristocracy and the Queen's family. This hope is destroyed in the one scene he has onstage. He can't recognise the hatred lingering behind their false protestations of goodwill.

Richard hypocritically plays up to Edward's delusion that he's 'Made peace of enmity, fair love of hate' (II.1.51) before announcing Clarence's death (II.1.81). In that moment, enmity and division return, Edward collapses in guilty grief, while Richard enjoys his 'tardy cripple' joke (91).

George, Duke of Clarence

Key quotes

'Simple plain Clarence' (Richard, I.1.118)
'... false, fleeting, perjured Clarence' (I.4.55)

Clarence is completely deceived by Richard's show of tears and professed love in I.1. His dream of being knocked overboard by Richard comes too late to alert him to the real source of danger; even when his murderers joke about Richard's brotherly love he can't believe them (II.4).

Dream stirs his conscience: he changed sides to help his brother after originally swearing loyalty to his Lancastrian in-laws – and then he killed the Lancastrian heir, Queen Margaret's son.

Motivated to commit crimes by 'My brother's love, the devil, and my rage' (I.4.226), Clarence knows he has put his soul in danger 'For Edward's sake' (I.4.68).

Richard's rivals

Prince Edward and Richard, Duke of York

Key quotes

'Two deep enemies,
Foes to my rest and my sweet sleep's disturbers' (Richard, IV.2.71–2)
'So wise so young, they say, do never live long' (Richard, III.1.79)
'I fear no uncles dead ...
An if they live, I hope I need not fear' (Edward, III.1.146–8)
'Bold, quick, ingenious, forward, capable.
He is all the mother's, from the top to toe.' (Richard, III.1.155–6)

Prince Edward is heir to the throne and Richard's main rival. He is a wary youth rather than the 'baby' of popular tradition. He is prepared to contradict Richard's view about dangerous uncles, and also initiates a serious discussion about history that gets under Richard's skin.

Edward's younger brother is Richard, Duke of York. York's affection for his 'kind uncle' contrasts with Richard's irritation that he is 'all the mother's'. His innocent joking about Richard's baby teeth (II.4.27-30), daggers and apes (III.1) can come across as mockery in performance (see Olivier's murderous stare at the 'ape' moment in his film).

Richard disposes of the threat posed by the two Princes when they are lodged in the Tower, visitor access is denied (IV.1), public information about their illegitimacy is accepted (III.7), Richard is crowned king (IV.2) and Tyrrel is hired to manage their disappearance (IV.2, IV.3). As 'wicked uncle', Richard has no pity or family feeling for them.

Henry Tudor, Earl of Richmond

Key quote

> 'Live, and beget a happy race of kings!' (ghosts of Princes, V.3.158)

It is significant that the dead Princes (who should have inherited the crown) identify Richmond as their heir. His distant Lancastrian claim to the throne is thus fortified by Yorkist approval even before he marries Princess Elizabeth.

Those opposed to Richmond accuse him of being a 'White-livered runagate' (IV.4.464), 'never trainèd up in arms' (V.3.273) and 'A milksop' (V.3.326). Richard tries to dismiss Richmond as no threat because he has no military experience. Richmond's reign as Henry VII is foreshadowed as a time of 'smooth-faced peace' (V.5.33).

Richard's victims

Duke of Buckingham

Key quotes

> 'My other self' (Richard, II.2.151)
> 'The deep-revolving witty Buckingham' (Richard, IV.2.42)
> 'Repays he my deep service
> With such contempt? Made I him king for this?' (IV.2.118–9)
> 'That high All-seer which I dallied with
> Hath turned my feignèd prayer on my head' (V.1.20–1)

Buckingham is in more scenes than anyone but Richard. He is an essential assistant and fellow 'actor' but never Richard's equal. A favourite word for Buckingham is 'deep' – but Richard is much deeper.

As a proud hereditary noble, he thinks he'll be the power behind Richard's throne since he 'made' Richard king. He doesn't realise that Richard has been manipulating him: we can see Richard's cunning in letting Buckingham make the running in tricky situations (like getting York out of sanctuary or turning the crowd's sentiment towards them).

His humiliation over the gift of an earldom and realisation of Richard's false friendship (IV.2) come too late to save him. He realises that Margaret's curse on his sneering (I.3) is about to be fulfilled as he accepts his mortal sin and execution (V.1).

Rivers, Grey and Vaughan

Key quotes

'… the Queen's sons and brothers haught and proud' (Third Citizen, II.3.28)
'Today shalt thou behold a subject die
For truth, for duty, and for loyalty.' (Rivers, III.3.2–3)
'Now Margaret's curse is fallen upon our heads' (Grey, III.3.14)

Richard targets Queen Elizabeth through these characters. Their chief fault for Richard is that they're upstarts, a vulgar 'new' aristocracy expecting to share power with old 'blood'. Their main scene is III.3, before their death.

As individuals they are not important, but pay attention to how they recall the sins of the past against the crown. Scene III.3 reminds us, at a central point of the play, that each action is heading towards retribution, the fulfilment of Margaret's curse.

Lord Hastings

Key quote

'O momentary grace of mortal men,
Which we more hunt for than the grace of God!' (III.4.96–7)

As a victim of his own comfortable illusions and careless sense of power, he ungraciously celebrates his enemies' misfortune. He is flattered and then betrayed by Richard's deceptive friendliness.

Derby (Lord Stanley)

Stanley is an important political survivor, who appears to be loyal to the Yorkists but has conflicting family interests in his Lancastrian wife and stepson, Henry Tudor (Richmond), which leads him to help Dorset escape from Richard. Note the suppressed tension in his conversation with Queen Elizabeth (I.3.19–29). Significantly, Stanley crowns the new king (V.5.3–7).

Historical note: Stanley's descendant was Ferdinando, Lord Strange, patron of Shakespeare's company of actors called *Lord Strange's Men* in the early 1590s. Some commentators have suggested that Shakespeare goes easy on Stanley's opportunism for obvious reasons.

Brackenbury

Key quotes

'With this, my lord, myself have naught to do' (I.1.97)
'I will not reason what is meant hereby,
Because I will be guiltless from the meaning' (I.4.94–5)

Unlike Stanley who uses ambiguity to survive in a difficult situation, Brackenbury is a perfect public servant – discreet, firm, unemotional and loyal to his master. Note how he refuses the women's access to the Princes (IV.1). His death at Bosworth is reported by Stanley and honoured by Richmond (V.5.14–15).

Catesby, Ratcliffe and Lovell

Richard's trio of loyal servants, immortalised in the seditious printed rhyme of 1484 which read: 'The Cat, the Rat and Lovell our Dog, Rule all England under the Hog' (author William Collingbourne was executed for treason). Shakespeare characterises Catesby as cunning and Ratcliffe as hard.

Richard and women

Richard's approach to Anne and later Queen Elizabeth appears lustful but his verbal seduction is not sexually motivated. For him all they represent are ways to enhance his political power. His characteristic approach to the older women who are no use to him, Margaret and his mother, is mocking. Their collective grief, which he has caused through murder, means nothing to him. See the notes on Misogyny in the Themes, Ideas & Values section.

Lady Anne

Key quotes

'Arise, dissembler' (I.2.184)
'... my woman's heart
Grossly grew captive to his honey words' (IV.1.78–9)
'I'll have her, but I will not keep her long' (Richard, I.2.229)

Even though she knows that Richard has murdered both her father-in-law and her husband, Anne submits to him – amazed at her susceptibility and blaming her weak 'woman's heart'.

Richard makes her feel guilty for her beauty which seduced *him*. She doesn't deny her looks but accepting his flattery makes her feel complicit in his repulsive wooing. Her long reply to Elizabeth's kindness (IV.1.65–86) reminds us of her rebounding curse which she thinks she has deserved for giving in to Richard.

Anne's only value to Richard is in being the Earl of Warwick's daughter and a Lancastrian. He consolidates his power through gaining her family's status. Once he has the crown he must discard her to achieve a more secure dynastic marriage with his royal niece.

Queen Elizabeth

Key quotes

'I had rather be a country servant-maid
Than a great queen, with this condition,
To be so baited, scorned and stormèd at' (1.3.106–8)

'Ay me! I see the ruin of my house.' (II.4.49)

'A care-crazed mother to a many sons,
A beauty-waning and distressèd widow' (Buckingham, III.7.183–4)

'Shall I forget myself to be myself?' (IV.4.420)

Ennobled through marriage and so having no aristocratic power base to defend her, Elizabeth knows that her security depends on Edward. His death, the arrest of her relatives and then the murder of her sons lead her to despair.

Key point

Richard and Buckingham speak disrespectfully about Elizabeth as an ageing widow. In Shakespeare's time, widowhood was not a disgrace in itself, although it could lead to poverty and exploitation. A more common stereotype found in drama was the comic lustful widow. This is how the widow Elizabeth Grey is characterised by the nobility – she seduced Edward to provide for her fatherless children. Widowed again by Edward's death, she becomes vulnerable to a similar charge of being ambitious for her family.

You could argue that the play vindicates Elizabeth's intelligence and care for her family by the way she defeats Richard when he seeks to marry Princess Elizabeth (IV.4). Is she one step ahead of him when she agrees to let him marry her daughter so that she can resume a royal title? Stanley suggests that she's already accepted Richmond for young Elizabeth (IV.5.7–8). Or is she, as Richard believes, a 'shallow changing woman' (IV.4.431) who changes her mind again?

Queen Margaret

Key quotes

> 'My charity is outrage, life my shame' (1.3.276)
> 'What! Were you snarling all before I came ...
> And turn you all your hatred now on me? (I.3.187–9)

The last Lancastrian queen, widow of Henry VI, brings onstage with her an ancient, destructive energy. Her cursing is integral to the play's structure of revenge and retribution, yet modern productions cut down her role or edit her out completely: there is no Margaret in either the Olivier or McKellen film.

Her words are certainly repetitive in I.3 and IV.4 but this contributes to the dramatic effect (see notes on curses, below). She's part of the savagery that will be purged away by Richmond; but her curses are also a warning and an instrument of divine retribution.

Margaret has been a killer and battle leader, unforgiving and cruel. Unlike the other women, she is not merely a victim of the men's war. Richard hates her because she mocked his captured father York, who cursed her – for Richard, Margaret only gets what she deserves (I.3.173–180).

Following Richard's lead, all the courtiers join in a pious chorus of condemnation – which she turns around by cursing each of them (195–213). Richard tries to mock her but she is as tough as him, and when she curses him with a conscience it sticks (221–6).

Duchess of York

Key quotes

> 'Alas! I am the mother of these griefs' (II.2.80)
> 'He is my son – yea, and therein my shame' (II.2.29)
> 'And I for comfort have but one false glass
> That grieves me when I see my shame in him.' (II.2.53–4)

You could argue that the saddest figure among the women in this play is the old Duchess of York, mother of Edward, Clarence and Richard. She witnesses one son destroying the rest and is unable to prevent the next generation, her grandchildren, from trusting their kind witty uncle (II.2 and II.4).

Like Elizabeth, she sees the destruction of her house but goes a step further by taking responsibility for giving birth to the diabolical cause of it. She's reminded that her womb is a 'kennel' from which 'hellhound' Richard has crept (Margaret, IV.4.47–8). He is prepared to slander her name to prove Edward's illegitimacy (III.5.85–93).

THEMES, IDEAS & VALUES

Power

This general theme incorporates a cluster of ideas about the ways in which power is desired and exercised. These relate mainly to the struggle over royal power but extend to questions of status, obedience and loyalty. The exercise of power includes moral ideas and values such as being truthful or trustworthy, using deception to achieve goals, and treating the law and oaths seriously.

The place of history in the present, questions of how the past is remembered and honoured, and ideas of fame (or infamy) are also crucial to an understanding of power. The play's moral premise is that 'all-seeing heaven' (Elizabeth's phrase) observes human action and brings just retribution to a society corrupted by power struggles when the time is ripe.

Royal power

Key quotes

'Take heed you dally not before your King' (Edward, II.1.12)
'I am unfit for state and majesty' (Richard, III.7.204)
'… the King's name is a tower of strength' (Richard, V.3.12)

As Edward's physical power wanes, so does his capacity to control discord at court. Hence his appeal to the royal family to remember that behind him is the greater power of 'the supreme King of kings' looking on (II.1.13), through whom monarchs in Shakespeare's time believed they derived power to rule on earth. However, Edward's depleted spiritual authority fails to intimidate the divided nobility.

Compare Richmond's spiritual authority as someone who (technically a usurper) dedicates himself as God's 'captain' to fight against 'a bloody tyrant and a homicide' to protect English rights (V.3).

Key point

If the ruler has god-given status, then usurpation becomes the worst crime against divine will. Richard (usurper of nephew Edward's royal right) believes that achieving the 'king's name' and wearing the crown is all he needs to do to be the king.

Ironically, Richard unconsciously tells the truth when he modestly plays being 'unfit' to the crowd. Richmond provides a startling image of Richard as 'A base foul stone' that is 'made precious by the foil [precious metal setting for a jewel]/Of England's chair [throne], where he is falsely set' (V.3.251–2). That is, the throne should be 'set' with a person worthy to sit on it.

Power to command obedience

Key quotes

'We followed then our lord, our sovereign king;
So should we you, if you should be our king.' (Rivers I.3.146)
'Unmannered dog! Stand thou, when I command!' (Richard, I.2.39)

Rivers attempts to deflect Richard's dislike and curry favour at the same time by making a reasonable point about following the ruler, whoever that might be. What's missing from his view is a discriminating sense of loyalty – should you obey the person who's the king just because he's king?

Everyone must make a choice about obeying the ruler. Brackenbury has a bland dutifulness, following royal orders precisely without disturbing his conscience. Lord Stanley, more politically alert to his own interests, appears to do what Rivers says, obeying Richard until he can openly give allegiance to Richmond. Contrast Hastings, whose clear view about obedience to '[his] master's heirs in true descent' (III.2.54) exposes him to danger.

Richard is sensitive to status, offended that the nobility is 'Held in contempt' while the Queen's family is ennobled (I.3.78–81). He expects obedience from the lowest servant to the highest nobleman, Buckingham, who has to support his new king to the throne. See Olivier's film – the minute Richard is named king he makes Buckingham kneel in homage (end of III.7).

The ruler must be strong

Key quotes

'Woe to the land that's governed by a child!' (Third Citizen, II.3.11)
'Insulting tyranny begins to jut/Upon the innocent and aweless throne' (Queen Elizabeth, II.4.51–2)

How does a ruler acquire and maintain status – through military strength? Family and peer support? Personal charisma? Wise rule? A combination of all these?

Key point

A major preoccupation in Shakespeare's time was the importance of having a strong, effective ruler prepared to control factions and quell civil unrest. A child ruler can only be as capable as the guiding adults around him. An adult ruler is always preferable for the very reason Elizabeth cites – an 'innocent and aweless' throne (ruler) has no power to enforce obedience and can be pushed aside.

Shakespeare presents Edward IV, the child Edward, Richard and Richmond for us to judge each one's fitness to rule. Richard wants secure power but offers only military bravado as a leader, despising 'weak ... peace' (I.1.24). Richmond, though, welcomes 'smooth-faced peace' (V.5.33) as a sign of the kingdom's return to calm security.

Power brings burdens and grief

Key quotes

'Princes have but their titles for their glories ...
There's nothing differs but the outward fame' (Brackenbury, I.4.78–83)
'Small joy have I in being England's Queen' (Elizabeth, I.3.109)
'Will you enforce me to a world of cares? (Richard, III.7.222)

To offset the envy ordinary people might feel towards powerful rulers, another idea about the downside of power circulated widely in the literature of Shakespeare's time. It concerns the unseen burdens of responsibility and private grief experienced by royalty. Brackenbury meditates on this theme after listening to Clarence's 'restless cares' (I.4).

Retaining royal power demands constant effort and sacrifice, bringing 'small joy' as Elizabeth knows. She reiterates the point to Richard even more forcefully (I.3.150–4) while Queen Margaret comments in an aside on her own 'joyless' title (I.3.154–5).

Treacherous words

Key quotes

'My tongue could never learn sweet smoothing word' (Richard, I.2.168)
'I never was nor never will be false' (Derby, IV.4.493)
'... your grace's word shall serve,
As well as I had seen, and heard him speak' (Mayor, III.5.61–2)

Richard's power stems from his mastery of language: the 'sweet smoothing word' he claims he can't learn is in fact his usual style. Everything he says conveys sufficient ambiguity to put potentially suspicious victims off-guard (Clarence, Anne and Hastings). He enjoys playing with double meanings (for example in the word 'naught', I.1), and we frequently hear his sinister implication behind a show of goodwill.

A sign of Richard's decline is that he loses his facility to deceive with language in Act IV, while others gain the power to defend themselves and the truth with words. For example, Stanley, who is committed to Richmond but playing for time, relies on ambiguity to avoid giving a direct answer when Richard challenges his loyalty (IV.4.493) – and his ploy works. In the same scene, Elizabeth fights Richard in patterns of wordplay that give her the moral advantage over his argument, as in 'cousins/cozened' (i.e. fooled, IV.4.223). No longer the controller of the word game, he gives way to irritation at her quickness: 'Be not so hasty to confound my meaning' (IV.4.262).

Plausible liars do terrible damage, especially if they are in positions of power and trust. You might argue that the Mayor betrays his official duty when he accepts Buckingham's report of Hastings's treason as equivalent to witnessing it for himself. But why should he doubt the truth of Buckingham's words? The play demonstrates several times how easily individuals can be deceived by those in power.

Faces and hearts

Key quotes

'I would I knew thy heart' (Anne, I.2.192)
'We know each other's faces; for our hearts
He knows no more of mine than I of yours,
Or I of his, my lord, than you of mine' (Buckingham, III.4.10–12)
'For by his face straight shall you know his heart' (Hastings, III.4.53)

In a play driven by Richard's dissimulation (false appearances), Shakespeare explores the discrepancy between outward appearance and inner motivation by metaphorically contrasting the public 'face' with the hidden 'heart'. Buckingham's speech about guessing Richard's thoughts (which he's confident he knows) fails to warn Hastings, who persists in his error of thinking Richard's face will reveal his heart.

Richard's face may be unattractive but, because words are his strength, he substitutes 'tongue' for 'face' when trying to convince Anne that his 'heart' is true. He asks her to listen to his words because his heart is 'figured in [his] tongue' (I.2.193). His words, like his face, hide the inner truth.

Hypocritical shows

Key quotes

'Come, cousin, cans't thou quake and change thy colour …
As if thou wert distraught and mad with terror?' (Richard, III.5.1–4)

'I can counterfeit the deep tragedian' (Buckingham, III.5.5)

Richard's other great source of power is his acting ability: among other performances, he turns on tears for Clarence, professes hurt feelings for being misunderstood at court, enjoys a joking intimacy with Hastings that switches to outrage at being 'bewitched', and displays a bashful piety to fool the citizens.

Richard's soliloquies invite an actor to play to the audience, and his comment about being 'like the formal Vice, Iniquity' (III.1.82) enhances the idea that he is consciously sharing a performance with watchers who are 'in the know' and will enjoy his clever mischief.

Key point

Beneath the idea of Richard as a successful 'actor' lies another idea about the power of theatre to influence us to believe a false show – sometimes accepting it so absolutely that we mistake it for reality. Shakespeare's theatre is a lawful deception – we suspend our disbelief in order to discover deeper things about life through the constructed 'reality' in scenes and characters.

History and memory

An ancient idea often restated is that 'those who forget the lessons of history are condemned to repeat them'. *Richard III* is partly a moral lesson about remembering the bloody history that resolved itself in Henry VII's Tudor peace.

How do people remember the past – through written records? Or by looking at 'bruisèd arms hung up for monuments' (Richard's memories, I.1.6)? The royal women hold dynastic history in their memories: repetition keeps grief alive until retribution has been made.

Historical truth

Key quotes

'Methinks the truth should live from age to age' (Edward, III.1.76)
'I say, without characters fame lives long' (Richard, III.1.81)

Young Edward's observation about truth living on is a moral statement: it 'should' live, whether history is recorded or passed on through memories and stories. However, nowhere is truth more problematical than in recorded history. Look back at Shakespeare's sources for Richard and the Tudor story, which he brought together in a public show confirming popular 'truth' as Elizabethans would have seen it.

Truth is less interesting to Richard than 'fame' which doesn't need formal records, because famous people leave their own trace. He makes up this idea to cover a sinister remark about Edward's cleverness. The boy follows through by agreeing that Caesar 'lives in fame, though not in life' (III.1.88) – it could be an epitaph for both Richard and the 'Princes in the Tower' (see the huge number of websites about them, for instance).

Remembering history

Key quotes

'... drown the sad remembrance of those wrongs' (Richard, IV.4.252)
'Harp not on that string, madam; that is past.' (Richard, IV.4.364)
'Harp on it still shall I till heartstrings break.' (Elizabeth, IV.4.365)

In the tense exchange between Richard and Elizabeth in IV.4, Elizabeth states that past wrongs blight any optimistic promise he can make about 'the time to come'. His offer to repair 'all the ruins of distressful times' (318) astonishes her.

Richard thinks that memories of bad events can be removed simply by offering gifts or equivalent substitutes for what's gone. A husband's murdered, a child's killed, a title's lost – he'll step in to supply a new husband, a new family and enhanced status. Similarly, he offers a simplistic remedy for Anne's complex grieving: 'The readiest way to make the wench amends/Is to become her husband and her father' (I.1.155–6).

History can help us learn how to avoid mistakes and grow differently – but paradoxically it also works to help those like Elizabeth remember great wrongs. Memory assists revenge by reminding us who did what to whom, and who needs to 'pay'.

Memory as a burden

Key quotes

'Dead life, blind sight, poor mortal-living ghost,
Woe's scene, world's shame, grave's due by life usurped,
Brief abstract and record of tedious days' (Duchess, IV.4.26–8)

The Duchess of York's language strains to express her unbearable grief for the Princes. In II.2 and IV.4, notice how Margaret, Elizabeth, Anne and the Duchess fulfil their roles as Plantagenet memory-keepers, burdened by their grief for what cannot be forgotten. Richmond's new energy is imperative to purge away the pain of these memories.

Oaths and curses

Key quotes

'Can curses pierce the clouds and enter heaven?' (Margaret, I.3.194)
'Bloody thou art, bloody will be thy end' (Duchess, IV.4.195)

Oaths are serious promises by individuals who call heaven to witness and to punish them should they break their word. Curses are malign wishes expressed in public, calling on heaven to cause the requested injury. In *Richard III*'s series of dramatic ironies, curses rebound on the curser (such as Anne and Hastings).

Richard's attempt to persuade Elizabeth to give him her daughter (IV.4) forces him to utter a sacred oath to prove his 'dear heart's love'. However, it sounds more like a curse on himself (IV.4.397–405) – and it rebounds just before battle.

Buckingham discovers too late that lightly-made promises about false friends return as punishments on oath-breakers. His extravagant oath of friendship to Elizabeth (II.1.32–40) is insincere but he can't imagine that what he wishes on himself will ever happen. Still less does he think that God hears curses (I.3.284–5).

Revenge and retribution

Key quotes

'Thus hath the course of justice wheeled about' (Margaret, IV.4.105)
'Plantagenet doth quit Plantagenet,
Edward for Edward pays a dying debt' (Margaret, IV.4.20–1)
'O God, which this blood mad'st, revenge his death!' (Anne, I.2.62)

Revenge is about getting even, a 'kind of wild justice' as one Elizabethan lawyer (Francis Bacon) described it. It satisfies a private desire for payback but is likely to incite another act of revenge in return. This is what the inter-family killings in the Wars of the Roses degenerated into, as Margaret's quotes show.

Anne's appeal to God for revenge reminds us that, in the Christian context of Shakespeare's time, human wickedness offends divinely ordained natural and social relationships. But is desire for revenge an approved Christian idea? What about forgiveness?

Retribution

Key quotes

'So just is God, to right the innocent' (Elizabeth, I.3.181)
'God will revenge it' (Richard, II.1.140)
'This, this All Souls' Day to my fearful soul
Is the determined respite of my wrongs.' (Buckingham, V.1.18–19)

Retribution means rewards and (especially) punishments. Divine retribution refers to God's rewards and punishments, particularly when a major crime against society has been committed, such as violating the sacred office of kingship by murder and usurpation. Divine retribution breaks the violent cycle of human revenge in a slow but sure working-out of justice for everyone.

The wicked may prosper for a time and the innocent may suffer, but vindication will come according to absolute moral principles. Richmond embodies God's will for a revived England; he bears 'bruising irons of wrath' (V.3.111) to fight his holy war, not just against Richard but to end the long dynastic squabble for the crown.

In Richard's dangerous world it is imperative for the human soul to be prepared for death, and the play makes this point in different ways. Hastings, Clarence and Buckingham are good examples:

- Catesby reminds Hastings (who is gloating over his enemies' fall, so does not really take any notice): 'Tis a vile thing to die … When men are unprepared and look not for it' (III.2.62–3).
- Clarence's murderers try to justify their deed by arguing that they're carrying out God's vengeance on him, and Clarence knows there is 'evidence against [his] soul'. As a final act of goodness he asks avenging God to spare his innocent wife and children (I.4.67–72).
- Buckingham thinks about 'all that have miscarriѐd/By underhand corrupted foul injustice' as he waits to die (V.1.5–6). He concludes that he is receiving what he deserves: 'Wrong hath but wrong, and blame the due of blame' (28–9).

Relationships

The play explores relationships in a damaged society, both between people and within the fragmented self. The destabilising consequences of dynastic wars are examined at the domestic level through the breaking of family and sibling bonds, friendships betrayed, curses exchanged and promises broken. Love is scorned or used as a weapon, pity is suppressed or warped into deceitful shows, conscience becomes associated with cowardice, and fearful minds are tormented by ominous dreams.

Family bonds broken through rivalry

Key quotes

'My husband lost his life to get the crown ...
And being seated, and domestic broils
Clean overblown, themselves the conquerors
Make war upon themselves, brother to brother,
Blood to blood, self against self ...' (Duchess of York, II.4.57–63)

'Your aery buildeth in our aery's nest' (Margaret, 1.3.269)

Richard's mother wearily sums up the self-defeating cruelty of family in-fighting that breaks the closest of human relationships. In contrast, Margaret's image of Yorkist birds of prey (eagles build aeries) usurping the Lancastrians' rightful family nest perpetuates the deep bitterness between them.

Richard touches suggestively on the almost incestuous closeness of sexual rivals sharing 'the selfsame name', 'Plantagenet' (I.2.142) as an invitation to Anne to simply substitute him for her murdered husband. Compare Richmond and Elizabeth: 'The true succeeders of each royal house' (V.5.30–1) negating Plantagenet rivalry (even though they're both Plantagenet descendants) in a new Tudor marriage.

Damaged brotherhood

Key quotes

'... our princely father York ...
... charged us from his soul to love each other,
He little thought of this divided friendship' (Clarence, I.4.238–41)

'... this deep disgrace in brotherhood
Touches me deeper than you can imagine' (Richard, I.1.111)

Sibling rivalry isn't a new idea but Shakespeare demonstrates how the bonds between brothers are eroded by one mischief-maker.

Clarence sentimentally believes Richard will respond to the memory of their father's battlefield blessing, but Richard has no need of brothers. Edward and Clarence stand between him and the crown so he simply eliminates them. Notice the ambiguity of his 'deep disgrace' comment to Clarence. Richard is actually telling him that he's responsible for his brother's disgrace ('touches me'), while implying that he finds Edward's treatment of his brother disgraceful.

Clarence's dilemma is common to many people living through a period of war: his split loyalties (to the Lancastrian Nevilles through marriage and to his Yorkist brother Edward) lead to his nightmare of underworld punishments.

Contrast this with how Richmond's good qualities are confirmed by his concern for his stepbrother's welfare before celebrating victory. His first question to Stanley, who has just handed him the crown, is: 'But tell me, is young George Stanley living?' (V.5.9).

Failure of friendship

Key quotes

'He hath no friends but what are friends for fear' (Blunt, V.2.20)

'And take deep traitors for thy dearest friends' (Margaret's curse, I.3.223)

'When I have most need to employ a friend,
And most assurèd that he is a friend,
Deep, hollow, treacherous and full of guile
Be he unto me!' (Buckingham, II.1.36–9)

'Dar'st thou resolve to kill a friend of mine?' (Richard, IV.2.68)

Richard III examines how affection, trust, honesty, loyalty, protectiveness and shared values – features of genuine deep friendship – can be destroyed by rivalry, fear and distrust.

Friendship is impossible in an environment where trust and human feeling have been eroded. Catesby pretends to be Hastings's friend to entrap him (III.2) and his friend Stanley hastily abandons him (III.4). Richard has no need of friends at all, identifying only 'many simple gulls' he can manipulate, like 'Derby, Hastings, Buckingham' (I.3.327-8).

While Buckingham's fatal mistake is to take Richard's intimacy for genuine friendship, he's also self-interested, expecting to be amply rewarded for being Richard's right-hand man. He's insulted in IV.2 to find that he is only a temporary companion in ambition.

Sorrowing women

Key quotes

'So many miseries have crazed my voice' (Duchess of York, IV.4.17)

'Tell over your woes again by viewing mine' (Margaret, IV.4.39)

'And often up and down my sons were tossed
For me to joy and weep their gain and loss' (Duchess of York, II.4.58–9)

Because the play deals with masculine power strategies in the struggle for ultimate patriarchal authority, the bearers of the royal title are always 'king'. In this scenario women inevitably become pawns or victims, without status even though they may have significant dramatic voices and royal titles. For more on this topic, read Madonne Miner's article '"Neither mother, wife, nor England's queen": The Roles of Women in *Richard III*' (see References & Reading).

If women are characterised principally as Plantagenet memory-keepers, their main dramatic role seems to be ritualised and repetitious, keeping dynastic wounds open but with no agency to act for themselves. Shakespeare does in fact give them more individuality than this; a common mistake of directors is to cut the play by editing down women's scenes.

Key point

Women who initially are bitterly divided discover a strange sisterhood through sharing their grief and extending pity to each other. Their memories may be unhealable – but they show how it is possible to curse and weep your way to fellow-feeling, to share another's sorrow because it is like your own.

Misogyny (hatred of women)

Key quotes

'Why this it is when men are ruled by women' (Richard, I.1.62)
'Your beauty was the cause' (Richard to Anne, I.2.121)
'I never looked for better at his hands
After he once fell in with Mistress Shore.' (Buckingham, III.5.49–50)
'Play the maid's part: still answer nay, and take it.' (Buckingham, III.7.50)

Although some male characters express misogynistic views, Shakespeare's play isn't inherently misogynistic; nor would Elizabethan audiences have been automatically polarised along gender lines in response to those views. Recent feminist criticism is essential to open discussion about power relations, gender and sexuality – but keep in mind the dramatic context in which views are expressed and any underlying motives of the character who expresses them.

Richard not only attacks women verbally but encourages Clarence and Buckingham to air their prejudices about Queen Elizabeth and Mistress Shore. We hear the full range of medieval Christian prejudices against women in criticism and jokes throughout the play.

Richard's opening soliloquy identifies peace with a weakening (feminising) of men and a dangerous reversal of masculine authority. His tone is both scornful (look how peace turns soldiers into women's playthings, dancers and lovers) and resentful (his deformed body isn't sexually attractive to any 'wanton ambling nymph'). Then Anne unexpectedly gives in to him, and he's shocked at her perversity – how could she want him after her young husband? (I.2.246–9). She later admits fault for allowing her 'woman's heart' to be so 'grossly' captured by him.

If women are to blame for men's sexual misbehaviour, then beautiful Anne can't refute Richard's argument. Neither can Jane Shore, who was still famous in Shakespeare's time and had plays and poems written about her. Clarence and Richard snigger at her sexual power over King Edward – heralds have to 'trudge' around all night (a verb suggesting heavy-footedness, as if they're worn out with carrying so many lovers' messages).

Buckingham follows Richard's theme when he conjures up a picture of Edward 'lulling on a lewd love-bed' (III.7.71) guaranteed to shock the respectable Mayor. After Richard attacks Hastings for defending Mistress Shore, Buckingham again draws the moral with prissy distaste (III.5.49–50).

Buckingham's joke about women's sexual availability masked by fake modesty, where 'no' is to be understood as 'yes' – 'still answer nay, and take it' (III.7.50) – is made even more repulsive when Richard picks it up. He turns it into a perverse joke about giving birth. He suggests that because he can't refuse Buckingham, he'll 'play the maid's part' and between them they'll 'bring it to a happy issue' (50–3) – just as the maid saying 'yes' might well end up with a baby.

Conscience

Key quotes

'Where's thy conscience now?'
'O, in the Duke of Gloucester's purse' (First & Second Murderers, I.4.128–30)
'[Conscience] fills a man full of obstacles' (Second Murderer, I.4.141)
'The worm of conscience still begnaw thy soul!' (Margaret's curse, I.3.221)
'O coward conscience, how dost thou afflict me!' (Richard, V.3.180)
'Conscience is but a word that cowards use,
Devised at first to keep the strong in awe' (Richard, V.3.310–11)

Many people would agree that having a conscience is essential for being morally and ethically aware – it connects us to the consequences of our actions, helps us to think before we speak or act and to reflect afterwards, possibly leading to an apology or correction. Conscience is an inner prompting – the old word for it was 'inwit' (inner knowing). We don't have to make public what it tells us, but we can listen to it for our own sake in a world where morality and ethics are often not valued.

Richard knows he's 'in/So far in blood that sin will pluck on sin' (IV.2.62–3) but can't stop. He sees conscience as merely a hindrance to action – interestingly, something that he misnames as 'cowardice' (because we know he isn't a coward). He's thrilled to have defeated Anne's 'conscience' (I.2.234) – as she admits later. He encourages Clarence's murderers to forget their consciences with bribery.

Margaret curses him with a conscience – and divine retributive justice activates it in his nightmare. As a result, Richard's *psychomachia* (battle in the soul) is a classic conscience debate (V.3.178–207).

Dreams, omens and prophecies

Key quotes

'Let not our babbling dreams affright our souls' (Richard, V.3.309)
'I have dreamed a fearful dream!' (Richard, V.3.213)

These affect people subconsciously and determine outward behaviour as well as beliefs about the supernatural. Dreams and nightmares are personal, although Carl Jung theorised that some dreams may also reflect a culture's disturbances and fears. Omens are often taken as warnings – Hastings remembers too late how his horse stumbled three times on its way to the Tower (III.4.84–5). Prophecies range from fortune-telling to genuine foresight. Richard thinks they have no underlying truth, because he's circulated his own 'drunken prophesies, libels, and dreams' (I.1.33). However, divine providence delivers genuine warnings to characters.

Clarence, Stanley, Richard and Richmond have prophetic dreams that symbolically represent what is about to happen as well as mirroring the state of the dreamers. Clarence and Richard have conscience-stricken dreams; Stanley takes his as a warning, while Richmond is comforted.

DIFFERENT INTERPRETATIONS

Different interpretations arise from different responses to a text. There is no single correct reading or interpretation of a text. However, an interpretation is more than an 'opinion' – it is the justification of a point of view on the text as a whole or on one element of it. To present an interpretation of the text based on your point of view, you must use a logical argument and relevant evidence from the text to support and strengthen it.

Explore a range of productions on film, including the latest from the RSC (2007 Season) with video clips. Then read some of the written comments from productions and actors. You'll find that the interpretive focus is mostly on three areas.

Richard's character

Is Richard a tragic man, a cold psychopath or an instrument of God's justice?

- Consider how you could justify a characterisation emphasising any of these interpretations. Research Olivier's playful, cruel schemer; Sher's 'bottled spider'; and McKellen's military dictator.
- John Bell modelled his Richard III (2002) on Colley Cibber's famous adaptation of 1700, which became more of a favourite than Shakespeare's original until the end of the nineteenth century. Bell created a 'Gothic' atmosphere with a stony dungeon set and lurid lighting, and he used Cibber's additional lines in his characterisation of Richard. (See the Bell Shakespeare Company website at www.bellshakespeare.com.au for further details and pictures.)
- Olivier also used Cibber material to make his opening soliloquy even longer and ended with 'Richard's himself again' before plunging into battle – so we don't feel too bad about his death.

Key point

One thing Shakespeare's Richard can't be is a misunderstood good man. You might well argue that the historical Richard was misrepresented by Tudor spin but his dramatic character has to be a villain.

Female characters

What individuality do the four women have if you read their lines carefully? Rather than editing them out or reducing them to a few lines of grief, think how you might represent them as key dramatic elements in Richard's 'world'.

- Are the women emotionally weak, unable to defend themselves in a violent physical world except by words? How can they wield words for maximum effect? The wooing scenes (Anne, Elizabeth) can be played as fiercely interactive – especially with Elizabeth.

- See the different approaches to Lady Anne's character playing to Olivier (Claire Bloom) and McKellen (Kristin Scott Thomas).
- Would you delete any of Margaret's lines? What would be the consequences of writing her out completely – as Olivier did?

Morality play

You could decide to either accentuate or cut down on religious elements for a more contemporary socio-political context. A religious fundamentalist Richard (from any major religion or sect) would be more about power and control than spirituality; another alternative is to start the play with a military coup, with Richard as the product of decadent times (McKellen). You could still bring out character dynamics and their corrupting interdependence – when one falls, they're all going to fall. The focus would be on the question of what social forces throw up a personality like Richard's – so obviously malign – that acquires power.

QUESTIONS & ANSWERS

The essay topics below show a range of possible styles and formats, and are suitable for senior English assessment tasks and examinations.

1 Richard is a great actor – so why can't he play the role of king successfully?
(Analyse the features and conventions used to construct Richard as a character; develop an interpretation.)

2 'Because Richard speaks his "honey words" to us as well as to Lady Anne, he charms us into accepting his villainy.' Discuss.
(Examine ideas and characters constructed and presented in the play.)

3 'The play shows that you cannot escape a bad conscience.' Discuss.
(Develop an interpretation; consider how the play is open to different interpretations.)

4 'The play demonstrates that immoral actions have inevitable consequences for the wrongdoer.' Discuss.
(Develop an interpretation; analyse values embodied in the play.)

5 What strategies do the women in Richard's world utilise to survive and exercise limited power?
(Examine ideas and female characters constructed and presented in the play.)

6 "Truly the hearts of men are full of fear" (Second Citizen, II.3.38). How does the play reveal what people will do when they are afraid?
(Consider ideas and characters presented; analyse values embodied in the play.)

7 How would you account for the change in Richard's character as the play develops?
(Consider how the play is open to different interpretations.)

8 'The play does not need Queen Margaret's curses because characters doom themselves by their own words and actions.' Do you agree?
(Consider ideas and characters presented by the play.)

9 '*Richard III* demonstrates that people are susceptible to being fooled by a cynical hypocrite because of flaws in their own character.' Discuss.
(Develop an interpretation of the play with close attention to characterisation.)

10 The Third Citizen says: "leave it all to God" (II.3.45). How important is human action shown to be in redressing wrongs?
(Develop an interpretation; analyse values embodied in the play.)

Analysing a sample topic

'*Richard III* demonstrates that people are susceptible to being fooled by a cynical hypocrite because of flaws in their own character.' Discuss.

Answer this question by choosing a few main characters (no more than three or four) to illustrate your argument. You're being asked to think of the interplay between Richard ('a cynical hypocrite') and, say, Anne, Hastings, Buckingham and Queen Elizabeth (a selection of 'people').

Think through the ideas about human nature being proposed in the question, which will form your opening sentences:

- A cynic is someone who assumes the worst about people – Richard assumes his victims can be led to believe anything through stupidity, fear, pride, selfishness, greed or other character weakness.

- Richard is a hypocrite – he has no problem with telling lies or presenting a false appearance.
- How would you define character 'flaws'? How can they make people vulnerable to exploitation? Is individual conscience important to keep people aware of what they are doing?

Preparatory notes for main discussion

List your character examples: beside each name, note how Richard fools them, e.g. seduces Lady Anne with words, reassures Hastings that he's a friend, gets greedy Buckingham to be his 'right-hand man', terrorises Elizabeth by killing off her family then offers to make amends by marrying her daughter.

Note each character's weakness, or whatever Richard thinks will win them over. Find short quotes to support your discussion. They tell you themselves when they reflect on their situation:

- Anne (IV.1) knows she's been weak to succumb to Richard's flattery (I.2) and betray her loyalty to the dead, going against her own conscience. She's half believed his claim that it was her 'fault' for seducing him merely by being attractive. Her self-cursed punishment is to endure a tormented, loveless marriage ending in her own murder.
- Just before his execution, Hastings (III.4) realises his error in thinking he is safe because he can discern Richard's heart (thoughts and feelings) in his face (outward demeanour), also while mocking his friend's warning and obvious bad omens (III.2, III.4).
- Buckingham, as the most powerful duke after Richard, is promised more rich favours (III.1), feels superior to Hastings as Richard's 'friend in the know' (III.2, III.4) and enjoys the dramatic game of manipulating foolish Londoners (III.7) to help Richard gain the throne. His pride and greed lead him to think he has made Richard king (IV.2.119), when in fact his trust in Richard's 'false faith' has been misplaced all along.
- Queen Elizabeth, alone of all Richard's victims discussed here, stands her ground while appearing to give in: Richard assumes she will as a 'shallow, changing woman' (IV.4.431). She signals that she's bought Richard's argument about making reparation for murdering

one family by creating a new one but, instead of repeating Anne's mistake, Elizabeth out-manoeuvres Richard – we find out from Derby that she's agreed to her daughter's marriage with Richmond (IV.5).

Conclusion

Reflect on the proposition in your conclusion. Your examples will confirm the view that some people's character flaws make it easier for them to be manipulated. You could point out finally that Richard's approach to men and women differs, even though his aim is to seduce them all with words: with Buckingham and Hastings he stresses collegiality, flattering their pride, whereas with the women, he targets their vulnerability.

SAMPLE ANSWER

'The play demonstrates that immoral actions have inevitable consequences for the wrongdoer.' Discuss.

Many characters in *Richard III*, both innocent and corrupt, die as a consequence of Richard's selfish plotting to gain the crown. The play certainly follows his many wrong actions against family and friends to his own fatal conclusion. Yet, while the consequences of immoral actions may be thought of as 'inevitable', implying that some divine moral justice exists, several characters come to understand their experiences in more complex terms than a simple distinction between innocence and guilt. The play thus encourages us to think about human responsibility for what happens in the world and how conscience comes into the picture.

An action could be defined as 'wrong' when it goes against a character's conscience, or contrary to what they know to be right in a particular situation. Lady Anne and Buckingham, for example, both contribute to their own downfall when they enable Richard to exploit them and then turn against them. These characters have a last chance to look into their own conscience to realise what they have contributed to their fate – in other words, to link immoral actions to inevitable consequences for them.

Although Lady Anne often arouses pity in an audience as an exhausted victim, she is an individual whose immoral action rebounds on the wrongdoer. She knows in her conscience that she's been emotionally disloyal at a crucial moment when she could have resisted Richard's seduction. She knows he has murdered her husband as well as her father-in-law, Henry VI, a rightful king he's also helped to depose. Yet even with Henry's body beside her and Richard's sword in her hand, she can't take revenge by killing him on the spot, because this would also be an immoral action for her. She accepts him because she can't resolve the moral dilemma, or so Richard encourages her to believe through his offer of a choice between the sword and himself.

Richard cruelly exploits what she believes about her own 'weak' personality – she has beauty as well as a fickle 'woman's heart' that 'grossly grew captive' to his false words. Her punishment is to know that she has betrayed her conscience for a loveless marriage, while her curse against Richard's wife rebounds as soon as she has uttered it.

Buckingham's wrong actions in bullying the citizens to support Richard, and lulling Hastings into a false sense of security, are more obviously political and public. When he draws a line at agreeing to the Princes' murder, Richard humiliates him and casts him off. On All Souls' Day, Buckingham waits to die and is reminded to take stock of his soul by examining his conscience. Like Anne, he falls victim to his own rhetoric – in his case, an insincere oath of loyalty, containing the wish for God's punishment of betrayal by a friend 'and most assured he is a friend' if he should break his word. Buckingham's last line shows that he accepts his fate because 'wrong hath but wrong, and blame the due of blame' – in other words, his fall is mostly due to his own wrongdoing.

The most spectacular arrival of 'inevitable consequences' for the wrongdoer is demonstrated in the parade of ghosts, all Richard's victims, uniting in a nightmare intended to demoralise him on the eve of battle. The result is his violent death, fighting bravely but alone and without any purpose other than to gamble his life.

Unlike Anne and Buckingham's more realistic heartfelt meditations on their actions, Richard's conscience is only temporarily activated. His refusal to respond to what he calls 'a word that cowards use' in any other way than to fight sets him apart from the play's other characters. He is a monstrous anti-social energy that can't take in the moral lesson the play has demonstrated, through Anne and Buckingham, about wrongdoing and its inevitable consequences.

REFERENCES & READING

Text

Shakespeare, William 2005, *Richard III*, ed. E. A. Honigmann, Penguin, London.

I suggest you also read Introductions to the Oxford and Arden editions for useful insights and background. See the Cambridge School Shakespeare edition (2006) for further useful text notes with glossary, reading activities and production photographs.

Criticism and background

Bullough, G. 1966, *Narrative and Dramatic Sources of Shakespeare Vol. III*, Columbia UP, New York.

Candido, J. 1987, 'Thomas More, the Tudor Chroniclers, and Shakespeare's Altered Richard', *English Studies*, vol. 68, no. 2.

Colley, S. 1992, *Richard's Himself Again: A Stage History of Richard III*, Greenwood Press, New York & London.

Davies, A. 1988, 'Laurence Olivier's *Richard III*' in *Filming Shakespeare's Plays*, Cambridge UP, Cambridge.

Day, G. M. 1991, '"Determined to Prove a Villain": Theatricality in *Richard III*', *Critical Survey*, vol. 3, no. 2.

Dessen, A. 1986, *Shakespeare and the Late Moral Plays*, University of Nebraska Press, Lincoln.

Loehlin, J. N. 1997, '"Top of the world, Ma": *Richard III* and cinematic convention' in L. Boose & R. Burt (eds.), *Shakespeare, The Movie*, Routledge, London, pp.67–79.

Miner, M. M. 1980, '"Neither mother, wife, nor England's queen": The Roles of Women in *Richard III*' in C. Lenz, G. Greene & C. Neely (eds.), *The Woman's Part: Feminist Criticism of Shakespeare*, Illinois UP, Urbana.

Richmond, H. 1989, *Shakespeare in Performance: King Richard III*, Manchester UP, Manchester.

Righter, A. 1967, *The Legacy of the Vice, in Shakespeare and the Idea of the Play*, Penguin, Harmondsworth, pp.86–91.

Rossiter, A. P. 1961, *Angel with Horns*, Longman, London. (See especially pp.1–22.)

Sher, A. 1985, *The Year of the King, an actor's preparation for the role*, Methuen, London.

Toole, W. B. 1974, 'The Motif of Psychic Division in *Richard III*', *Shakespeare Survey* 27, pp.21–32.

Film

Richard III 1956, dir. Laurence Olivier. Starring Olivier as Richard.

Richard III 1995, dir. Richard Loncraine. Starring McKellen as Richard.
Also read Ian McKellen's Introduction to the Richard III *screenplay (Transworld, 1996).*

Shakespeare: The Animated Tales Richard III 1994.
Slight and abridged but useful to hear Anthony Sher voicing Richard.

Looking for Richard 1997, directed by and starring Al Pacino.
An actor-director's exploration, popular but only marginally useful as a study guide – it's really about Pacino's struggle to 'find' his character ... any character.

Websites

http://www.npg.org.uk/live/search
National Portrait Gallery, London, will show you all known portraits of historical Richard III.

http://www.rsc.org.uk
Royal Shakespeare Company, UK, has details, reviews, photos of recent Richard III *productions and extensive archives of earlier productions.*

http://www.richardiii.net
Website of Richard III Society, UK, gives details of continuing lively interest, debate and activities related to Richard and his times.